ANTHRACITE REGION

KEYSTONE TOMBSTONES

JOE FARRELL AND JOE FARLEY

WITH LAWRENCE KNORR

SUNBURY
PRESS

Mechanicsburg, Pennsylvania   USA

Published by Sunbury Press, Inc.
50 West Main Street
Mechanicsburg, Pennsylvania 17055

www.sunburypress.com

For information about special discounts for bulk purchases, please contact Sunbury Press Orders Dept. at (855) 338-8359 or orders@sunburypress.com.

To request one of our authors for speaking engagements or book signings, please contact Sunbury Press Publicity Dept. at publicity@sunburypress.com.

ISBN: 978-1-62006-554-9 (Trade Paperback)

Library of Congress Control Number: 2015933673

FIRST SUNBURY PRESS EDITION: April 2015

Product of the United States of America
0 1 1 2 3 5 8 13 21 34 55

Set in Bookman Old Style
Designed by Crystal Devine
Cover by Lawrence Knorr
Edited by Allyson Gard

Continue the Enlightenment!

INTRODUCTION

This special edition of the **Keystone Tombstone** series centers on the graves of the famous and infamous that are buried in the Anthracite Region. The purpose of this volume is to bring to the readers attention grave sites worth visiting in the area. In addition, we hope to make the trips easier and most convenient. For that reason, the chapters are separated by county to allow for planning multiple visits.

For those of you new to the series, each volume of **Keystone Tombstones** contain mini-biographies of various people of note who have been laid to rest in Pennsylvania. We include photos of the individuals, monuments or places important to their story, as well as the graves and the tombstones. At the end of each chapter, we have an "If You Go" section where we recommend other graves in the vicinity you may want to visit as well as local eating establishments and watering holes where you can refresh yourself. We've received plenty of positive feedback relative to these sections in the books.

As far as potential places to visit, the Anthracite Region offers a varied menu. You've got a man many consider to be the greatest athlete ever in Jim Thorpe. The world of entertainment is represented by Jayne Mansfield, Zane Grey, and Nick Adams. You have two women whose stories involve the Kennedys with Mary Jo Kopechne and Mary Pinchot Meyer. Pennsylvania politicians are represented by Dan Flood and Bob Casey. Finally, in addition to many others, two stories dealing with Pennsylvania history are told in chapters on the Molly Maguires and the Lattimer Massacre.

One of the things we have found is that visiting these sites can be a very educational experience. It is our hope that you come away from reading this volume and visiting the sites with a similar feeling. While we have tried to make locating the cemeteries and graves as easy as possible, we recommend that you visit the cemetery office when possible, to request assistance in locating the graves. Take it from us, this can save you a lot of time.

So we wish you the best on your visits and we hope you find them fulfilling. At the sites, feel free to leave some mementos (grave goods) in memory of the individual who have passed. It's always nice to find these on our visits. Finally, we hope you enjoy this volume and we encourage you to check out the other books in the series.

Joe Farley

CONTENTS

"The Greatest Athlete of the 20th Century"

JIM THORPE

County: Carbon
Town: Jim Thorpe
Cemetery: Jim Thorpe Memorial
Address: 101 East 10th Street

The man who many consider to be the greatest athlete of his time is buried in Pennsylvania in the town that bears his name. Jim Thorpe excelled at multiple sports, though he is best remembered for his accomplishments in football and in track and field. It was as a direct result of his play in these two areas that from 1996-2001 he was awarded ABC's Wide World of Sports Athlete of the Century award.

Thorpe was born on May 22, 1888 in Oklahoma on a Sac-and-Fox Indian reservation. Thorpe's youth, not unlike his adult life, was filled with ups and downs. His father recognized his athletic ability and encouraged young Thorpe to develop it. Among his favorite childhood games was chasing (on foot) and catching wild horses. He was also a big fan of follow the leader, though when he was the leader you would have to do things like climb trees and jump to the ground as well as swim across rivers. Thorpe was also known to run the 20 miles home from school each day. He thrived at competing with others.

As mentioned above, there were also childhood disappointments. Few in his family were blessed with long lives. His twin brother passed away when he was 8. Both of his parents died when he was in his teens. He took his father's death extremely hard.

When Thorpe was 16 he was recruited to attend the Carlisle Indian School in Carlisle, Pennsylvania. It was here that his athletic ability caught the attention of the legendary coach Glen "Pop" Warner. One day Thorpe was walking past the field where the track team was practicing. He stopped to watch and noticed how no one could clear the high bar that was set at 5 feet 9 inches. Despite the fact that he was in his street clothes, he walked onto the field and cleared the height easily.

Jim Thorpe

Thorpe enjoyed great success in track and field while attending Carlisle. For example, in 1909 he almost beat the Lafayette team by himself when he won six events. The Lafayette coach, Harold Anson Bruce, said he had never seen such a natural athlete. But it was on the football field where Thorpe really made a name for himself. Pop Warner was initially against Thorpe playing football because he felt his star track and field athlete might get hurt. Finally, Thorpe convinced him to let him run a few plays in practice. On two successive plays Thorpe galloped for touchdowns untouched. After the exhibition, Thorpe walked over to Warner tossed him the football and said, "Nobody is going to tackle Jim."

By 1911, Pop Warner was calling Thorpe "the greatest all-around athlete in the world." That year, Carlisle was to play the powerful Harvard football team in Cambridge. Thorpe was outstanding at running the ball, using his strength and remarkable speed to consistently advance its position. One reporter noted that he was amazing at avoiding tacklers in the open field. Thorpe was responsible for all of Carlisle's points. While scoring a touchdown and kicking four field goals, he led his team to a 18-15 upset win. Thorpe's play during the season earned him All-American honors.

While 1911 was a great year for Thorpe, it could not compare to his accomplishments in 1912. The 1912 Olympics were held in Stockholm that summer and Thorpe was a member of team USA. First he won the pentathlon a competition that included five different events. Six days later he competed in the decathlon where he set a world record with 8,412 points. What is remarkable about this total is that if Thorpe had posted the identical marks in the 1948 Olympics he would have won the silver medal. In fact his time of 4 minutes 40.1 seconds in the 1500 meter race would not be beaten until the 1972 Olympics.

After his Olympic performance he was congratulated by King Gustav V of Sweden. The king told Thorpe, "Sir, you are the greatest athlete in the world." Thorpe replied, "Thanks, king."

Thorpe returned to the United States as a national hero. New York City honored him with a ticker tape parade.

Jim Thorpe as a member of the New York Giants.

At the conclusion of the parade Thorpe remarked, "I heard people yelling my name and I couldn't realize how one fellow could have so many friends."

That fall he returned to Carlisle to resume his football career playing for Pop Warner. One of the teams he faced was Army, whose roster included a cadet named Dwight Eisenhower. Carlisle won easily 27-6, and Thorpe put on a spectacular performance. On one play, he galloped 92 yards for a touchdown only to have the play nullified due to a penalty. On the next play he went 97 yards for the score. His play obviously impressed the future president who spoke of Thorpe in a 1961 speech. Ike said, "Here and there, there are some people who are extremely endowed. My memory goes back to Jim Thorpe. He never practiced in his life, and he could do anything better than any other football player I ever saw."

Carlisle went undefeated in 1912 and was widely acknowledged as the national champion. Thorpe won All-American honors again and he found himself sitting on top of the athletic world. There was, however, trouble on the horizon.

A writer for the Worcester Mass. Telegram named Roy Johnson published a story stating that Thorpe had been paid to play semi-pro baseball in 1909 and 1910. During this time, it was not unusual for college athletes to play semi-pro, but most played under different names to avoid losing their amateur status. Thorpe made the mistake of playing under his real name.

As a result of this revelation, the Amateur Athletic Union asked Thorpe for an explanation. Thorpe replied in writing saying, "I hope I will be partly excused by the fact I was simply an Indian schoolboy and did not know about such things. I was not very wise in the ways of the world and did not realize this was wrong." There was not at the time any good reason for not accepting Thorpe's explanation. The Athletic Union thought otherwise and withdrew Thorpe's amateur status retroactively. The International Olympic Commission followed suit by declaring Thorpe a professional athlete. As a result, Thorpe was stripped of his Olympic titles and his gold medals. Almost immediately Thorpe began receiving offers from professional teams.

In 1913 baseball was the most popular sport in the country. It was also, arguably, Thorpe's weakest sport. He signed with the New York Giants where he played in the outfield for three seasons. Thorpe played six seasons of professional baseball, from 1913 to 1915 and from 1917 to 1919. His career totals in baseball are unimpressive. He played in 289 games and had a career batting average of .252. He scored 91 runs and drove in another 82. His career in the big leagues was over though he did continue to play minor league ball until he hung up his bat and glove for good in 1922.

Professional football was in its infancy and nowhere near as popular as it is today. That didn't stop Thorpe from signing with the Canton Bulldogs in 1915. The Bulldogs paid Thorpe $250 per game an amount that in current dollar terms would exceed $5,000. This was considered a very lucrative wage. At the time, Canton's average attendance per game was about 1,200 fans. When Thorpe made his debut, 8,000 paying customers attended the game. Thorpe and the Bulldogs were successful in winning league titles in 1916, 1917, and 1919. With little time left in the 1919 title game, the Bulldogs were forced to punt from deep in their own territory. Thorpe, with the wind at his back, took the snap and kicked a 95 yard punt sealing the victory and the championship.

While playing for the Bulldogs, Thorpe was named the league's President, a post he held for one year. He continued to coach and play for Canton until he joined the Oorang Indians in 1921. He was with this team, made up of all Native Americans, through 1923. While the team did poorly, Thorpe played well enough to be named to the first ALL-NFL team in 1923. Thorpe never won an NFL championship and retired from football in 1928 at the age of 41.

It was recently discovered that Thorpe also had a basketball career. In 1926, he was the star player for the "World Famous Indians" of Larue. His team played exhibitions in New York, Pennsylvania, and Ohio. The fact that he was a basketball player came to light in

Jim Thorpe at 1912 Olympics

2005 when a ticket to one of his games was discovered in an old book.

After Thorpe's athletic career ended, he led a troubled life. His first two marriages, which produced eight children, ended in divorce. One son, Jim Jr. died at the age of two. Thorpe's drinking, which had always been a problem, grew worse. It was not unusual for his drinking binges to end in fights. He also found holding a steady job difficult. He worked many odd jobs that included painting, digging ditches, serving as a deck hand, and a bar bouncer. In the 1930's he appeared in a few short films, usually playing an Indian.

By 1950, Thorpe was broke. That same year, the nation's press named him the most outstanding athlete of the first half of the 20th Century. He did receive about $15,000 from Warner Brothers in 1951 when the movie "Jim Thorpe All-American" was released. The film starred Burt Lancaster in the role of Thorpe and was a big hit.

In 1953, Thorpe was living with his third wife in a trailer in Lomita, California. While eating dinner on March 28th Thorpe suffered his third heart failure. Artificial respiration was used, and it revived him for a short time before he died. He was 64.

Here is the final resting place (at least for now) of the man that was called the greatest athlete in the world.

Another section of the Jim Thorpe Memorial that tells the story of his life.

Thorpe's athletic achievements have been recognized by many organizations. In 1951, he was elected to the College Football Hall of Fame. In 1963 he was named a Charter Enshrinee in the Pro Football Hall of Fame. He is also a member of the Track and Field Hall of Fame. In 1986, the Jim Thorpe award was created. It is awarded annually to the best defensive back in college football.

After his death, supporters of Thorpe pushed to have his Olympic titles reinstated. Thirty years later their efforts proved successful. On January 18, 1983, commemorative medals were presented to Thorpe's children. He was once again declared an Olympic champion.

In 1954, the towns of Mauch Chunk and East Mauch Chunk merged to form the town now known as Jim Thorpe. Town leaders made a deal with Thorpe's third wife to have his remains moved there in 1954. The town erected the Jim Thorpe Memorial which currently house the great athlete's remains. In June of 2010, Thorpe's son Jack filed a federal lawsuit seeking to have his father's remains retuned to Oklahoma. The case is pending.

If You Go:
See "Molly Maguires" on page 100.

COLUMBIA COUNTY

"Johnny Yuma Was a Rebel"

NICK ADAMS

County: Columbia
Town: Berwick
Cemetery: Saints Cyril and Methodius Ukrainian
Address: Crystal Hill Road

He was an actor who appeared in a number of significant films including "Mister Roberts," "Giant" and "Rebel Without a Cause." He was nominated for an Academy Award for Best Supporting Actor in the 1963 film "Twilight of Honor," but the award went to Melvyn Douglas. He is best known for playing the role of Johnny Yuma in the television series "The Rebel." His name was Nick Adams.

Adams was born Nicholas Aloysius Adamshock on July 10, 1931, in Nanticoke, Pennsylvania. His father, Peter Adamshock, was a Ukrainian born coal miner. When Adams was five years old, his uncle was killed in a mining accident, and as a result, Adams's father moved the family to Jersey City, New Jersey.

Peter Adamshock got a job as a janitor in an apartment building. One of the jobs perks was that it came with living quarters in the basement. During this period Adams's mother went to work for Western Electric.

When young Nick was still in high school, he received an offer from the Saint Louis Cardinals to play minor league baseball. He turned that offer down because he didn't feel the job paid enough. It's been said that as a teenager he made money by hustling pool games. Money was obviously important to him. When his father urged him to pursue a trade, he responded by saying he wanted to do something where he could make a lot of money and that he couldn't do that with a trade. So it could be said that the pursuit of wealth is what led to his decision to get into acting.

In 1947 Adams, who was 17 at the time, visited New York City. He went into a theater where an audition was being held for a play called "The Silver Tassie." It was here that he met the actor Jack Palance who, like Adams, hailed

Photo of Nick Adams in a guest-starring role on the television program The Monroes.

from the coal country of northeastern Pennsylvania and was of Ukrainian descent. When Palance asked Adams why he wanted to be an actor the answer he got was for the money. Palance, who had changed his name from Jack Palahniuk, introduced Adams to the director as Nick Adams. Adams failed to land a part in the play, but

Palance directed him to a junior theater group where he got an acting job playing the role of Muff Potter in "Tom Sawyer." During this time, Adams auditioned for a role in the play Mister Roberts where he met the legendary actor Henry Fonda. Fonda advised Adams to take some acting lessons. After a year in New York City, Adams hitchhiked across the country to Los Angeles.

Once he reached Los Angeles, Adams worked as a doorman, usher and maintenance man at the Warners Theater in Beverly Hills. His first paid acting job was in a stage play called "Mr. Big Shot." His first film role came in 1951 in a movie titled "Somebody Loves Me." The following year he was drafted into the United States Coast Guard.

In June of 1954 Adams auditioned in his Coast Guard uniform for the famed director John Ford. The effort earned him the part of Seaman Reber in the film "Mister Roberts." Adams completed his military service and upon his return to Los Angeles, based on his work in "Mister Roberts," he signed a contract with the Warner Brothers studio.

In 1955 Adams landed a role in the movie "Rebel Without a Cause" He befriended the stars of the movie James Dean and Natalie Wood. During breaks in the filming Dean and Adams would entertain the cast by imitating movie stars such as Marlon Brando. When Dean was killed in an automobile accident in 1955, Adams overdubbed some of Dean's lines for the film "Giant." Adams attempted to cash in on Dean's death by writing articles about Dean for movie magazines. In addition he claimed that he had adopted Dean's habits when it came to fast cars, claiming he had been arrested for speeding nine times in one year.

In the late 1950s, Adams' career began to blossom. He appeared in a number of successful television shows such as "Wanted: Dead or Alive" which starred Steve McQueen. In addition he appeared in films including "No Time for Sergeants" and "Pillow Talk."

In 1959 Adams was cast to star in a television series titled "The Rebel." Adams's character was named Johnny Yuma, an ex-Confederate soldier who wandered through the west toting a sawed off shotgun. Adams had hoped to get his friend Elvis Presley to sing the title song for the show, but the producer picked Johnny Cash. The show was a hit and 76 half-hour episodes were filmed before it was canceled at the end of the 1961 season.

In 1964 Adams appeared in an episode of the television show "The Outer Limits." Critics would later point to this performance as proof that he was underrated as an actor. In 1964 he co-starred in the movie "Young Dillinger" but the critics panned the movie and it flopped.

It was around this time that Adams' career began to go downhill. In 1965, after publicly declaring that he would not work on films that were produced outside the United States, he accepted parts in Japanese science fiction films including "Frankenstein Conquers the World" and the 6th Godzilla film "Invasion of Astro-Monster." During this peri-

Unique grave of the underrated movie and TV star Nick Adams.

od he also starred in a film with Boris Karloff that was filmed in England called "Die, Monster, Die!" In 1967 Adams would appear in a Disney release titled "Mosby's Marauders." He also appeared in a number of television series including "The Wild Wild West" and "Combat." In 1968 he was cast to star in a low budget science fiction film called "Mission Mars" which critics described as being "utterly dreadful." His last production in the United States was a stock car movie titled "Fever Heat." His last appearance on film was in a Spanish language western called "Los Asesinos."

Adams married a former child actress named Carol Nugent in 1959. The couple had two children, Allyson Lee Adams and Jeb Stuart Adams. The relationship between Adams and his wife was a rocky one. By 1965, they were separated, and the children were living with Carol. In November of 1966 Carol initiated divorce proceedings and obtained a restraining order against Adams.

On the night of February 7, 1968 Adams failed to show up for a dinner appointment he had made with his lawyer Erwin Roeder. Roeder drove to Adams Beverly Hills home to check on the actor. He broke a window to gain entry and found Adams in his upstairs bedroom in a sitting position leaning against a wall dead. Adams was 36 years old.

The coroner Dr. Thomas Noguchi determined that the cause of death was "paraldehyde and promazine intoxication." He was unable to determine if the death was accidental or a suicide. Over the years Adams' children have speculated that foul play may have been involved in the death of their father. Adams' best friend, actor Robert Conrad, has always felt that the death was accidental. Adams was laid to rest in the Saints Cyril and Methodius Ukrainian Cemetery in Berwick, Pennsylvania.

Adams' death at such a young age has made him part of what's been called the curse of "Rebel Without a Cause." The curse is based on the fact that four of the cast members of that film passed away at a very young age. As mentioned previously, in addition to Adams, James Dean died in an automobile accident at the age of 24. Another star in the movie was Sal Mineo who was stabbed to death on February 12, 1976 while he was walking home from a rehearsal for a play. He was 37 years old. Finally the female lead in the movie, Natalie Wood, drowned on February 28, 1981. Wood was 43 years old at the time of her death.

If You Go:
The authors suggest a visit to "The O'Donnell Winery" located at 25 Hayes Road in Berwick. The wines are tasty, and the owners are very friendly and eager to do all they can to meet your needs. In addition, weather permitting there is outside seating in a beautiful setting where you can watch the Susquehanna River flow by as you enjoy the fine wines.

The authors with Norbert O'Donnell, the owner of the O'Donnell winery in Berwick.

"Half the Horsemen"

JAMES (JIM) CROWLEY and HARRY STUHLDREHER

Counties: Lackawanna, Allegheny
Towns: Moscow, Pittsburgh
Cemeteries: Saint Catherine's, Calvary
Addresses: Route 435 and Main Street, 718 Hazelwood Avenue

On October 18, 1924, the famed sportswriter Grantland Rice was covering the Notre Dame–Army football game. After Notre Dame's 13-7 win, Rice authored what may well be the most famous sports story lead off ever written. It began,

> "Outlined against a blue-grey October sky, the Four Horsemen rode again. In dramatic lore their names are Death, Destruction, Pestilence, and Famine. But those are Aliases. Their real names are Stuhldreher, Crowley, Miller, and Layden. They formed the crest of a South Bend cyclone before which another fighting Army team was swept over the precipice at the Polo Grounds this afternoon as 55,000 spectators peered down upon the bewildering panorama spread out upon the green plain below."

With Rice's inspiration, a Notre Dame student publicity aide named George Strickland, made sure the name stuck. When the Irish team arrived back in South Bend he placed the four players, dressed in their uniforms and each holding a football, on four horses he obtained from a local stable. The famous photograph was quickly picked up by the wire services, and the legend of the Four Horseman of Notre Dame became forever embedded in the hearts and minds of American sports fans.

The horsemen were put together by the legendary coach Knute Rockne. They are widely considered to be the greatest college football backfield in the history of the game. They appeared in 30 games together and won all but two. Both losses were at Nebraska. In 1922, the Cornhuskers prevailed 14-6. They followed that with a 14-7 win in 1923.

The Four Horsemen of Notre Dame—Don Miller, Elmer Layden, Jim Crowley and Harry Stuhldreher

Playing at Notre Dame in 1924, the horsemen sought their revenge and succeeded, winning 34-6. They remain the only college backfield where all four members were voted into the College Football Hall of Fame. Two of the four, Jim Crowley and Harry Stuhldreher are buried in Pennsylvania.

Jim Crowley was born on September 10, 1902, in Chicago, Illinois. Shortly after his birth his family moved to Wisconsin. He picked up football by playing at Green Bay East High School. He was coached at the time by a man named Curly Lambeau. Lambeau would go on to found the Green Bay Packers.

Crowley graduated from high school and in 1921 enrolled at the University of Notre Dame. He went out for and made the football team. Coach Rockne, known as "The Rock", nicknamed him "Sleepy Jim" because of his droopy eyelids and his laid back demeanor. This latter trait I would come to witness 48 years later. Rockne saw he had some talented young players and he decided to make a backfield out of them. Though none of the four were taller than six feet or weighed more than 162 pounds, the Rock placed Crowley at left halfback, Don Miller at right halfback, Elmer Layden at fullback, and in charge of it all, Stuhldreher at quarterback.

Notre Dame contended for the national title in Football in both 1922 and 1923. In both years, however, losing to Nebraska ended those hopes. In 1924 there was no way of denying the Irish the title. Only two teams, Army and Northwestern, came within a touchdown of beating Notre Dame. In addition, Rockne decided that Notre Dame would play in the Rose Bowl against a powerful Stanford squad. Stanford was coached by the legendary Pop Warner and was also undefeated, though they did have one tie. The Stanford team was led by the great Ernie Nevers at quarterback and they dominated the game offensively if one looks at the statistics. However, the statistic that mattered most, the final score, was 27-10 in Notre Dame's favor. The Irish intercepted 5 Stanford passes, and returned 2 for touchdowns. Layden (who returned both interceptions for scores) and Crowley both made outstanding plays in the Irish victory. Notre Dame was declared the National Champion. The game marked Notre Dame's first appearance in a bowl game. They would not play in another until 1969.

The year 1924 proved to be Crowley's best at Notre Dame. He led the team in rushing yards and in scoring. He was also named to the All American team along with his teammates Layden and Stuhldreher.

After graduation, Crowley had a short professional football career, playing in just three games for the Green Bay Packers and the Providence Steamrollers. In 1925, he made his last appearance as a player when he took the field for the Waterbury Blues. He was joined in the backfield by his former teammate and fellow horseman Harry Stuhldreher. The Blues won the game 34-0 and Crowley scored three touchdowns. Following the contest, he picked up his check and left the team.

While his playing days were behind him, Crowley was not done with football. First, he became an assistant coach at the University of Georgia. In 1929 Michigan State hired him to be their head coach. His head coaching debut proved successful as he led Michigan State to a record of 22-8-3 in four seasons.

At the time, Fordham University was a college football powerhouse. In 1933, Crowley left Michigan State to coach Fordham. His success continued. He turned Fordham into one of the top defensive teams in the country. In 1936, he made future Notre Dame coach Frank Leahy his defensive line coach. Crowley and Leahy developed a line that would become famous. The line earned its own nickname, the "Seven Blocks of Granite." One of the blocks was none other than Vince Lombardi, who would go on to have considerable success coaching in the National Football League.

In 1939, a Crowley coached Fordham team appeared in the first televised football game. In that game, Fordham easily defeated the Waynesburg Yellow jackets by a score of 34-7. Crowley's last game at Fordham was in the 1942 Sugar Bowl. His team defeated Missouri 2-0. Crowley left Fordham after compiling a record of 56-13-7.

In 1946, a new professional football league, the All-American League, was established. Crowley became its first commissioner. Crowley resigned that position after one year to become part owner and head coach of the worst team in the league, the Chicago Rockets. His pro coaching career was a short and unsuccessful one. In 1947, his team went 1-13 and he hung it up as a coach prior to the 1948 season.

With his football career over Crowley moved to Pennsylvania to become an insurance salesman. In 1953, he relocated to Scranton, Pennsylvania to become station manager and sports director of an independent television station. In 1955 he was named chairman of the Pennsylvania State Athletic Commission. He remained as chairman until 1963.

Crowley was inducted into the College Football Hall of Fame in 1966. At the time, he was making a living as an after dinner speaker at various banquets. In 1969 he was the speaker at my high school team's basketball dinner. Here he demonstrated how Rockne came to nickname him "Sleepy Jim." While his stories were very humorous his expression and the tone of his voice never changed. In addition, the droopy eyelids were ever present and perhaps

Very modest gravesite of the quarterback of the legendary Four Horsemen of Notre Dame.

even more pronounced than they were when he was a younger man. I do recall him saying that there was one problem with being a member of the four horseman. He said whatever you did after that didn't matter. You were always one of the horsemen. He swore that he could have been governor of a state and that he would still be introduced as one of the four horsemen.

Jim Crowley was the last surviving horseman. He died in Scranton on January 15, 1986. He was 83 years old. He is buried in a very modest grave in Saint Catherine's Cemetery in Moscow, Pennsylvania.

Harry Stuhldreher was born on October 14, 1901 in Massillon, Ohio. It was here he spent his formative years. At the time Massillon fielded a professional football team. The star of the team was none other than a man by the name of Knute Rockne. There are stories that Stuhldreher would carry Knute's gear for him as a way to get into the games.

Stuhldreher's family moved to Pennsylvania where he played football for and graduated from the Kiski School in the town of Saltsburg. After graduation, he decided to attend the University of Notre Dame. There are those who believe this decision may have been influenced by his earlier interactions with Rockne.

Whether the gear carrying stories are true or not is open to speculation. One thing that isn't is that Rockne identified Stuhldreher as the man who would lead what became the most famous offense in college football history. He was very small for a football player standing at 5 feet 7 inches and

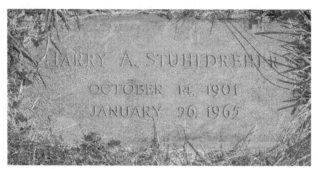

Very modest gravesite of the quarterback of the legendary Four Horsemen of Notre Dame.

weighing all of 151 pounds. His contemporaries described him as cocky and ambitious. Rockne saw him as a leader.

As detailed earlier, the four horsemen experienced tremendous success at Notre Dame. We already covered the 1925 Rose Bowl where the Irish bested Stanford. What is not well known is that early in that game, Stuhldreher broke his ankle. He refused to leave the game. In spite of the injury, he played a key part in the Irish win.

Stuhldreher later told stories about that 1924 Notre Dame team. He said that at one point, Rockne was concerned that the Horsemen were getting all the credit for the wins and that the line (now known as the seven mules) was a second thought. According to Stuhldreher, Rockne called the team together for a vote. "Which is more important to this team," he asked, "the line or the backfield?" According to Stuhldreher the line won by a vote of 7 to 4.

Very much like Crowley and his fellow horsemen, Stuhldreher went into coaching after his college playing days were over. His first job was at Villanova University. He was head coach there for 10 years starting in 1925, and he compiled a record of 65-25-9. Based on this success, he was hired by the University of Wisconsin as both head football coach and athletic director.

His tenure at Wisconsin had its ups and downs. While he coached the Badgers to be the Big Ten runner-up twice, there were unsuccessful seasons mixed in. At the time, as they do today, Wisconsin fans took their football seriously. During a bad year, the local newspaper printed a letter to the editor. The writer said, "We have a great offensive coach at one of our high schools and a great defensive coach at the other. What we need to do is fire Stuhldreher and hire these two guys as co-coaches." That evening when Stuhldreher arrived home from work, his oldest son was waiting for him newspaper in hand. He was angry. He demanded to know if his father had read the letter. Stuhldreher admitted he had, and, trying to calm his son down, basically said that you have to expect these things when it's not going well. His son responded, perhaps in jest, "Heck those two guys are bums. *My* coach is the guy that should have your job."

Stuhldreher wrote two books. One was called "Knute Rockne, Man Builder." The book was used as a source for the movie "Knute Rockne All American" that starred Pat O'Brien and Ronald Reagan. The film gave Reagan his nickname, the "Gipper."

Stuhldreher left Wisconsin for Pittsburgh to join U. S. Steel in 1950. In 1958, he was inducted into the College Football Hall of Fame. On January 26, 1965, he died in Pittsburgh of acute pancreatitis. He was 63. He is buried in a modest grave in Calvary Cemetery in Pittsburgh Pennsylvania.

The Four Horsemen remain a major part of the tradition that is Notre Dame Football to this very day. The Notre Dame bookstore continues to market shirts, sweats, cups, and glasses that show the famous photo of the horsemen atop their steeds. Every year, the students and alumni of the university sponsor a game day shirt. These same students, and many others, wear this shirt to every home game. The 2011 shirt has the picture of the Four Horsemen on the front. In light of all that the horsemen have contributed to Notre Dame, we were surprised at how simple and modest their grave sites remain. In Stuhldreher's case, we had to visit the cemetery office twice to get directions before we could find it. On our second trip, the office worker told us that Stuhldreher was under memorialized. We agree and note that there are Notre Dame clubs all over the Commonwealth. In our opinion, perhaps a couple of these clubs should take on the task of finding a way to honor these two horsemen in an appropriate manner.

Perhaps no one summed up the horsemen better than the legendary sportswriter Red Smith. Ironically, Smith was a friend and protégé of Grantland Rice. After Stuhldreher's death, Smith acknowledged all that the four had accomplished after leaving Notre Dame. Then he put it all together. He wrote, "Yet it was as a unit, and as undergraduates, they made their greatest contributions. They gave the game something special and precious that can't be coached and can't be manufactured. People call it romance."

If You Go:
Should you choose to visit Jim Crowley at Saint Catherine's, there are a couple of other graves you may want to visit. Former Pennsylvania Governor Bob Casey is buried there and so is Patrick DeLacy who was awarded a Congressional Medal of Honor. You are also in the vicinity of two other cemeteries covered in this volume (See page 30 on Congressman Dan Flood and page 34 on Mary Jo Kopechne). In addition, the area has many other attractions including quality golf courses, a triple A minor league baseball team, a major concert venue, and more than a few fine dining establishments. We recommend a visit to Woodlands Inn and Conference Center. The Woodlands offers multiple bars and eating establishments. The rooms are reasonably priced. You may also want to look into their vacation packages.

Should you visit Harry Stuhldreher at Calvary Cemetery you can find a number of gravesites worth seeing. Frank Gorshin (See *Keystone Tombstones – Pittsburgh Region*, p. 19), the actor best known for his role as the "Riddler" on the Batman TV series is buried here. Another actor, Gene Lyons, who is best remembered for playing Commissioner Dennis Randall, on the show "Ironsides" is interned here. So is David Lawrence (See *Keystone Tombstones – Pittsburgh Region*, p. 30), former Mayor of Pittsburgh and Governor of Pennsylvania. The Hall of Fame boxer Harry "The Human Windmill" Greb, is here as well. Speaking of boxers the light heavyweight champion from 1939-1941, Pittsburgh's own Billy Conn, was also laid to rest here. Of course there is plenty to do in Pittsburgh. There is a first rate amusement park known as Kennywood and the city also has a fine zoo. When we made our trip, we took in a Pirates game. They have a beautiful ballpark and we had a great time.

"The Three Time Loss from Holy Cross"
ROBERT CASEY

County: Lackawanna
Town: Moscow
Cemetery: Saint Catherine's
Address: Route 435 and Main Street

He had run unsuccessfully for the office of Governor of Pennsylvania three times before he won the 1986 election. He practically went to war with his own party over the issue of abortion, a procedure he staunchly opposed. In 1993 he underwent a controversial and rare heart-liver transplant. His name was Robert P. Casey.

Casey was born on January 9, 1932, in New York City. His family was originally from Scranton Pennsylvania, and they would eventually return there. Casey attended Scranton Preparatory School where he excelled as an athlete on both the baseball and basketball teams. As a matter of fact after he graduated, the Philadelphia Phillies wanted to sign him to a contract, but he decided to accept a basketball scholarship and attend college at Holy Cross. After graduation Casey went to George Washington University where he earned a law degree.

In 1962 Casey was elected to the Pennsylvania State Senate as a democrat from Lackawanna County. In 1964 he was present at the party's Saint Patrick's Day dinner where Robert Kennedy made his first public appearance since the assassination of his brother. In 1966 he made his first run for governor. Although he was the choice of the party professionals he was defeated in the primary election by Milton Shapp. He would repeat the loss to Shapp in 1970 and in 1978 he was defeated in the primary by Pete Flaherty. He was successful in both 1968 and 1972 when he was elected to the position of Pennsylvania's Auditor General.

Even though he was unsuccessful in his runs for governor, the name Bob Casey was popular among Pennsylvania voters. In 1976 a man who was also named Bob Casey ran for the office of State Treasurer. Although he spent little money and hardly campaigned at all he won the election.

Robert Patrick Casey, Sr. (January 9, 1932 – May 30, 2000) (Photo taken by Michael Casey)

In 1978 yet another Bob Casey won the Democratic party's nomination for the office of Lieutenant Governor.

The real Bob Casey had left his post as Auditor General because of term limits. He spent the next decade practicing law. In 1986 he decided to run for Governor of Pennsylvania for the fourth time. Many called him the three time loss from Holy Cross. Casey hired two virtually unknown political strategists to plan his campaign. Their names were James Carville and Paul Begala. Billing himself as the real Bob Casey, he won the Democratic primary. In the general election, he faced Pennsylvania's Lieutenant Governor, a son of a previous Pennsylvania Governor by the name of Bill Scranton. Needless to say whoever won the election would hail from Scranton, Pennsylvania. Most pundits would predict that Scranton would emerge the winner in the general election.

John Baer, in his excellent book *On the Front Lines of Pennsylvania Politics,* explains what he felt made the difference in the election. Baer agreed to work for Scranton as his press secretary. It is his view that the election was decided by three events. According to Baer, the first occurred in the state capital newsroom where Scranton appeared before reporters to deliver uplifting economic news showing that Pennsylvania was moving in the right direction. Toward the end of the press conference Scranton was asked about his endorsement of Bob Casey for Auditor General in 1972. At the time Scranton was running three weekly newspapers in the Pennsylvania northeastern coal region. Scranton responded by basically saying that one of the nice things about getting older was moving past your youthful indiscretions. Another reporter asked a follow up question saying speaking of youthful indiscretions any comment on drug use. Scranton left without answering the question. Within a few hours the press was all over the story. Eventually he admitted that in his youth he used recreational drugs.

According to Baer, the second pitfall took place when Scranton decided to take the high road and cease any negative political advertising. Initially the strategy appeared to work as the Scranton campaign received media praise. Then it all fell apart when the campaign sent out a direct mailer to 600,000 Pennsylvanians charging that Casey ignored fraud and corruption in state government while he was auditor general. The ad also claimed that during this period Casey was making $100,000 practicing law rather than attending to his public duties. The latter part of the ad was false as Casey made the money over a four year period. The story was picked up by Pennsylvania newspapers, and the Casey campaign labeled Scranton a hypocrite.

Scranton took the Casey campaign's final punch on the Friday before Election Day. Casey and Carville began airing what would become known as the "guru ad." The ad attacked Scranton for practicing transcendental meditation and included a 1960's picture of the lieutenant governor wearing long hair, a beard and tie-dyed clothing. Because the ad began airing so close to Election Day, Scranton was unable to respond to it. When the dust cleared, Casey was elected governor by a margin of about 79,000 votes.

Casey was inaugurated on January, 20, 1987. Casey called for an "activist government," and he favored expanding health care for women, reforming the welfare system, educational opportunities and environmental improvements. In his first budget he gave legislators a $12,000 raise, and he also raised his own salary. Despite the fact that he had raised their salary, his relationship with the state lawmakers was not a smooth one. At one point he publicly chided the legislature for their inaction on programs he favored. As detailed in John Baer's aforementioned book on one occasion Casey invited some legislators to the Governor's mansion for cocktails in an attempt to better relations. He asked a lawmaker named Bob O'Donnell what the problem was. O'Donnell told Casey, "There are two kinds of Irish: those that breed the poets, the drunks and the politicians; and those that breed the priests. We are mostly the former. I'm afraid you, lad, are the latter."

Casey was known for his strong stand against abortion. In 1989, he succeeded in passing the "Pennsylvania Abortion Control Act" which placed limitations on abortions. Planned Parenthood filed suit naming Casey as the defendant. The case went all the way to the United States Supreme Court where in June of 1992, the court upheld all of Pennsylvania's abortion restrictions except one. In addition, the court affirmed the rights of states to restrict abortion.

In 1990, Casey was easily reelected beating Barbara Hafer who was Pennsylvania's Auditor General at the time. Hafer made headlines when she called Casey "a redneck Irishman." Hafer did correctly predict that the state would face a billion dollar deficit in 1991. As a result Casey's next budget included $2.86 billion in new taxes.

Since Casey felt that abortion would be an important issue in the 1992 presidential election, he wanted to make a speech at the Democratic National Convention on the issue. The convention managers refused to give him a speaking slot, and Casey complained that he was being censored due to his pro-life views. After the convention, Casey went on vacation, and many thought he did so to avoid campaigning for Bill Clinton.

Yet another example of how important Casey felt the abortion issue was occurred in 1991 when one of Pennsylvania's Republican Senators, John Heinz, was killed in a plane crash. As Governor, it was Casey's job to appoint someone to fill the vacancy. He settled on a former aid to

Here is the grave of a man who finally won the office of Pennsylvania Governor by running under the slogan "The Real Bob Casey."

President John F. Kennedy named Harris Wofford. Casey extracted two promises from Wofford before he made the appointment. First, when he ran to be elected to the office he would choose James Carville to manage the effort, and second on the issue of abortion Wofford would support the Pennsylvania Abortion Control Act. With those promises, Casey actively supported Wofford in the special election held that fall when he defeated former Pennsylvania Governor Richard Thornburgh. After that election, Casey urged Wofford to support a legislative amendment which was similar to the Pennsylvania law. Casey threatened to withdraw his support in the next election if Wofford went the other way. Wofford supported the amendment but was defeated anyway in the 1994 election by Rick Santorum. Casey's oldest son would take the seat from Santorum in the election of 2006.

Early in his second term Casey was diagnosed with hereditary amyloidosis. It's a rare disease that had just a few years before claimed the lives of Pittsburgh Mayor Richard Caliguiri and Erie Mayor Louis Tullio. Casey's condition was made public just a few days before he underwent a rare heart-liver transplant on June 14, 1993. As a result many felt that Casey had been given preferential treatment by being moved ahead of others who were on organ donor waiting lists. For any family that has ever had a family member on such a list, it would be difficult to come to a different conclusion. Today there is an organ donation trust fund named in his honor. After the transplants, Casey continued to suffer from the effects of the illness, and he passed away on May 30, 2000. He was laid to rest in Saint Catherine's Cemetery in Moscow, Pennsylvania.

If You Go:
Should you choose to visit Bob Casey at Saint Catherine's, there are a couple of other graves you may want to visit. James Crowley (p. 15), one of the four horsemen of Notre Dame, is buried there, and so is Patrick DeLacy who was awarded a Congressional Medal of Honor. You are also in the vicinity of two other interesting cemeteries covered in this volume (See page 30 on Congressman Dan Flood and page 34 on Mary Jo Kopechne). In addition, the area has

many other attractions including quality golf courses,
a triple A minor league
baseball team, a major concert venue, and more than a
few fine dining establishments. We recommend a
visit to Woodlands Inn and
Conference Center. The
Woodlands offers multiple
bars and eating establishments. The rooms are rea-
sonably priced. You may
also want to look into their
vacation packages.

Jim Crowley (College Football Hall of Fame)

LUZERNE COUNTY

"Dapper Dan"

CONGRESSMAN DAN FLOOD

County: Luzerne
Town: Wilkes Barre
Cemetery: St. Mary's
Address: 695 North Main Street

Daniel Flood was born in Hazleton, Pennsylvania in 1903. He attended schools in Wilkes-Barre, a city where he would become a hero in later years. He earned a law degree from the Dickinson School of Law in Carlisle, Pennsylvania and began practicing law back in Wilkes-Barre in 1930.

Flood fancied himself an actor and, in fact, did appear on stage in local theatre productions and on various vaudeville stages. Some believe that his dabbling in acting was the foundation for his political style. He was nothing if not flamboyant, with a waxed moustache that curled up at both ends and a preference for all white suits sometimes complete with a cape. In addition, his speaking style drew comparisons to Shakespearean actors.

This author, who lived in the Congressman's district in the 1970's, heard him speak on two very different occasions. The first time took place in 1972 at Bloomsburg State College where he was the keynote speaker at a mock Democratic Convention. Congressman Flood was clearly annoyed by the reception he received (he was ignored by virtually all present). He had only begun his speech when he began waving his arms as he shouted into the microphone "I'm a United States Congressman and I deserve respect." This statement resulted in a combination of boos and laughter and the Congressman quickly cut his speech short and left the podium. This author heard him again in 1977 at a Friendly Sons of Saint Patrick's dinner in Hazleton. As you might imagine the reception was far different. Flood arrived at the dinner wearing one of his many white suits (with a green tie of course) and the crowd erupted in applause as he took his place at the main table. He gave a rousing speech about all the great things the Irish had done in America that was interrupted numerous times by

President Kennedy (left) with Congressman Daniel "Dan" Flood on the steps of the White House.

applause. At its conclusion he left the hall to a standing ovation.

Flood was first elected to Congress in 1944 but he was defeated in '46. He won again in 1948, but lost the seat in the huge republican sweep in 1952. He regained the 11th district seat in 1954 and after that was reelected 12 consecutive times, often without any real opposition. From

1954 on, Flood amassed the power that made him a mover and a shaker in Washington.

House Speaker Sam Rayburn took a liking to Flood and he quickly rose into leadership roles on important Congressional committees, including subcommittee chairman of the powerful House Appropriations Committee. He used his power and influence to divert federal dollars back to his district. Two of the major pieces of legislation he sponsored were the Area Redevelopment Act of 1961 and the Federal Coal Mine Health and Safety Act of 1969. In addition, the Interstate Highway System was under construction at this time and Congressman Flood saw to it that Interstates 80 and 81 intersected in his district. In fact, it's the only place in the country where the super highways meet.

The year 1972 brought both a challenge and opportunity to Flood when Hurricane Agnes caused massive, believe it or not, *flooding* in his district. The Congressman in the aftermath of the storm is said to have remarked "this will be one Flood against another." He used his clout to get monies through the federal bureaucracy that would normally have been held up. He also pressured authorities for air and boat rescue. He was successful in securing both. He convinced President Nixon to survey the damage which resulted in the President's involvement in the federal response. In the flood's aftermath, his popularity soared.

This was the highpoint of the Congressman's career. As he grew older, health problems slowed him down and he relied more heavily on his staff. In 1979, Flood was indicted on federal bribery and conspiracy charges. A member of the Congressman's staff was the chief prosecution witness. Some have put forward the proposition that the aide turned on Flood to save his own skin, though there is no concrete proof. However, as a result of the allegations, Flood resigned from Congress on January 31, 1980. The case was resolved with Flood pleading guilty to one count of conspiracy for which he was sentenced to one year of probation. Congressman Flood died on May 28th 1994. He was 91 years old. He is buried in Saint Mary's Cemetery in Wilkes-Barre. His grave is easily located as it sits on the left side of the road if you use the main entrance to Saint Mary's.

Here lies Congressman Dapper Dan Flood, who took on the flooding caused by Hurricane Agnes as if it had been personally aimed at him.

If You Go:

Also buried in Saint Mary's cemetery is Pete Grey who played major league baseball in 1945, despite having only one arm. Grey had lost his arm in an accident during his youth, but he continued to play baseball learning to throw and hit using his left arm. In the majors, Grey played in 77 games and had 51 hits in 234 at bats. To locate his grave, the authors suggest that you visit the cemetery office to obtain directions. In addition, if you are at Saint Mary's there is another cemetery in the area in the area you may wish to visit. Mary Jo Kopechne is buried in Saint Vincent's Catholic Cemetery located in Larksville (See page 34). You should also check out the "If You Go" section of "Half the Horseman," page 22.

"What If?"

MARY JO KOPECHNE

County: Luzerne
Town: Larksville
Cemetery: Saint Vincents
Address: Washington Avenue

The subject of this chapter is different than anyone else appearing in this volume. Mary Jo Kopechne is famous as a result of the way she died. Virtually everyone else in the book gained their fame through the things they accomplished while living. It is a fact that nobody can say how different America, and for that matter, world history might have been had Kopechne lived.

Mary Jo Kopechne was born in Wilkes-Barre, Pennsylvania on July 26, 1940. While she was still an infant, her family relocated to New Jersey. In terms of her education through High School, she was a product of the parochial school system. When it came time to choose a college Mary Jo decided on the Caldwell College for Women which is also located in New Jersey. She graduated in 1962 with a degree in business administration.

After graduation, Kopechne's first job was teaching at the Mission of Saint Jude in Montgomery, Alabama. In 1963, she moved to Washington, D. C., to work for Florida Senator George Smathers. Smathers was a close friend of John F. Kennedy, and he may have assisted Mary Jo in moving to Robert Kennedy's staff when he was elected Senator by the people of New York in 1964.

Kopechne was a loyal Robert Kennedy employee right up until the time of his death. When Kennedy decided to run for president in 1968 she went to work on his campaign. She worked with a group of women that became known as the "Boiler Room Girls", a nickname the six women earned because the office they worked in was hot and had no windows. Among their duties was tracking democratic delegates and how they intended to vote. One of the states that fell under Kopechne's responsibility was Pennsylvania.

Mary Jo Kopechne, far left during 1967 staff meeting with RFK.

On June 5, 1968, Robert Kennedy was assassinated. Kopechne was devastated and, at first, claimed she couldn't return to Washington. However, in December 1968, she was hired by Matt Reese Associates, a political consulting firm based in Washington. Through her work for the firm she soon found that she was on her way to a successful career.

By this time, Robert Kennedy's younger brother and senator from Massachusetts, Edward Moore Kennedy was already being mentioned as a potential candidate for president in either 1972 or 1976. Edward was commonly known as Ted or Teddy Kennedy and he had already turned down the chance to be a vice-presidential candidate in 1968. Many political pundits held the opinion that it was just a matter of time until the youngest of the Kennedy brothers would be elected president.

On July 18, 1969, Ted Kennedy hosted a party on Chappaquiddick Island, just off the Massachusetts coast to

honor the Boiler Room Girls. It is impossible to say with
any certainty what happened that night and in the early
morning hours of the next day. According to Kennedy, at
about 11:15 p.m. he indicated he was going to leave the
party. He said that Kopechne asked him if he could drop
her off at her hotel. Kennedy then obtained the car keys
from his chauffeur. When asked why he didn't have the
chauffer drive them both he said that the chauffeur was
finishing his meal and he didn't see a reason to disturb
him. Kennedy and Kopechne left the party. Mary Jo did not
inform her friends she was leaving and she failed to take
either her purse or her hotel key with her. Kennedy said he
was driving the car, a 1967 Oldsmobile, when he took a
wrong turn onto Dike Road. He said he was driving at
about twenty miles an hour when he came to a wooden
bridge known as Dike Bridge that had no guardrails. Immediately before reaching the bridge Kennedy hit his
brakes and then drove off the side of the structure. His car
ended up upside down underwater in Poucha Pond.
Kennedy said he escaped the vehicle, though he could not
remember how. He called out for Kopechne and getting no
response he claimed he repeatedly dove into the water but
that his attempts to reach the vehicle were unsuccessful.
He then said that he rested for a time before returning on
foot to the Lawrence Cottage, where the party was being
held.

According to his testimony, Kennedy denied seeing any
houses with their lights on as he walked back to the party.
According to others, he would have passed four houses on
his way back to the party. The first of these residences was
known as "Dike's House." It was 150 yards from the bridge.
Sylvia Malm, who was living there at the time stated that
she had left lights on in the house when she retired for the
evening and that she had a working telephone. There was
also a working telephone in the Lawrence Cottage.

The men at the party included Kennedy cousin, Joseph
Gargan, and a friend of Gargan's named Paul Markham.
According to Kennedy, he, Gargan, and Markham returned
to the scene of the accident. Again attempts by all three
men to reach the vehicle were unsuccessful. Gargan and
Markham then drove Kennedy to the ferry landing though

the last ferry had left for the evening. Both told Kennedy he needed to report the accident. Reportedly Kennedy responded, "You two take care of the girls, and I will take care of the accident." He then dove into the water, swam across the 500-foot channel, and returned to his hotel room. Gargan and Markham later took the position that they did not report the accident because they assumed Kennedy was going to do it.

At 8 a.m. the following day Gargan and Markham arrived at Kennedy's hotel room. According to his testimony, Kennedy said the two asked him why he had not reported the accident. He claimed that as he swam the channel he began to believe that somehow it would be found out that Mary Jo had survived. The three men then took the ferry back to Chappaquiddick where Kennedy made calls to friends, from a pay phone, requesting advice. The accident remained unreported.

That morning, fishermen spotted the automobile submerged in the water. They went to a nearby cottage and the residents notified the authorities. It was about 8:20 a.m. The Edgartown Police Chief James Arena, responded arriving in about 15 minutes. When his attempts to examine the interior of the vehicle were unsuccessful, he called a diver and a truck with towing capability. The diver, a man named Jim Farrar, arrived dressed in his scuba gear and recovered Mary Jo's body in about 10 minutes. He also checked the license plate and found that it was registered to Kennedy.

Shortly, the news reached Kennedy that the car and Mary Jo's body had been discovered. At this point, he took the ferry back to Edgartown and went to the police station to report the accident. When he arrived at the station, he made a few more phone calls before submitting a statement to the police. The statement, much of which has been covered above, created more questions than it answered.

Seven days after the incident, Ted Kennedy pleaded guilty to leaving the scene of an accident after causing injury. Judge James Boyle sentenced Kennedy to two months in jail but he promptly suspended the sentence, citing Kennedy's unblemished record. In his remarks, the judge noted that Kennedy "would continue to be punished beyond anything this court could impose." No one knows whether the judge was referring to the guilt Kennedy would be required to carry, or to the damage done to his political career.

There are many unanswered questions from the incident. Jim Farrar, the diver who recovered Mary Jo's body, claimed that her death was caused by suffocation and not by drowning. He said Kopechne had positioned her body to take advantage of an air pocket in the vehicle. It was his belief that if he had been called to the scene in a timely manner Mary Jo would have survived.

There is yet another interesting possibility as to what took place that night. A deputy sheriff by the name of Christopher "Huck" Look was working as a special officer that night due to the various celebrations related to the

Here lies a woman whose death may have changed American and World history.

Edgartown Regatta. He was driving home at about 12:40 a.m. when he saw a parked car containing a man and a woman stopped on a private road. Thinking the couple might be lost he went to offer assistance. He stopped his vehicle and at a distance of twenty to thirty feet began walking toward the car. The car started up and moved by him quickly. Look later recalled that the license plate contained an "L" and two "7"s a description that matched Kennedy's vehicle.

There are those that have put forth the theory that after eluding the deputy sheriff, Kennedy left the car and walked back to the party. Meanwhile, Kopechne, being unfamiliar with the area, drove off the bridge instead of returning to the party. The proponents of this theory argue that it accounts for Kennedy's lack of concern until the vehicle was discovered.

Whatever actually happened, it altered Kennedy's political life forever. While the people of the Bay State never turned on him, many of those outside Massachusetts never really trusted him again. He did not run for the presidency in 1972 or 1976. When he did run in 1980 against an incumbent president who was a member of his own party, he failed. In running against Kennedy, President Jimmy Carter often repeated that "he had never panicked in a crisis." For the remainder of his life Ted Kennedy remained the senior senator from Massachusetts. By all accounts he served his state well and was well respected by his fellow senators.

Mary Jo Kopechne died when she was just shy of her 29th birthday. She is buried in Saint Vincent's Cemetery in Larksville, Pennsylvania. As you enter the cemetery, you will notice a main section that makes its way up a modest hill. Mary Jo is about a quarter of the way up right in the middle of the main section.

If You Go:
You are close to the final resting places of two people covered in this volume. See page 30 on Congressman Dan Flood and page 15 titled "Half the Horsemen" on Jim Crowley.

"The Lattimer Massacre"

MICHAEL CHESLOCK

County: Luzerne
Town: Hazleton
Cemetery: Hazleton
Address: 120 North Vine Street

On September 17, 1897, the *Hazleton Daily Standard* published the following verse:

> If the courts of justice shield you
> And your freedom you should gain,
> Remember that your brows are marked
> With the burning brand of Cain.
> Oh, noble, noble, deputies
> We always will remember
> Your bloody work at Lattimer
> On the 10th day of November.

The verse was a testament to yet another act of violence involving labor and management in the anthracite coal region of Pennsylvania. This incident became known as the Lattimer Massacre.

The coal region is located in northeastern Pennsylvania. It is largely made up six counties: Lackawanna, Luzerne, Columbia, Carbon, Schuylkill and Northumberland. Coal was discovered in the area in 1762. This discovery would have a profound influence on those who chose to settle in the coal region in the 1800's. The coal industry went through a tremendous growth spurt after the civil war. This growth provided tremendous wealth for the few who had the capital to obtain mining rights and the land beneath where the vast deposits of coal could be found. For a minority of people who worked for the mining companies it provided a good job and a decent income. These people were mine bosses, superintendents, and supervisors. The majority of the employees were the actual miners who were faced with extremely dangerous work, harsh conditions and low pay coupled with the fact that they were forced to live in company supplied housing and purchase their

Mine workers marching to their slaughter outside of Lattimer, PA, September 10, 1897.

goods at company owned stores. Often a miner's wages failed to cover his and his family's expenses, and he went into debt to the company. These conditions led to conflict, sometimes violent, between labor and management (see "The Molly Maguires," p. 100).

The jobs in the mines were generally filled by the latest groups of immigrants to enter the region. This meant that in the 1890's most of the miners were of Italian or Slavic decent. At this time the company owned town of Lattimer housed an Italian population. Similar company owned towns in the area were largely occupied by Slavic miners and their families. In either case they were renting their homes from mine owner Ariovistus Pardee, who was one of the wealthiest men in America at the time.

As newcomers, these miners were often assigned the most difficult and dangerous jobs available. In addition, they were often subjected to prejudice. For example the Slavic miners were often called "hunkies." They were also angry about the "alien tax" that had been passed by the Pennsylvania General Assembly. This tax required a three-cent levy per day on all immigrant employees. When one considers that the immigrants' earnings were already set lower than their more established counterparts doing the same work, it becomes easy to see the anger that resulted from these conditions. Thus the stage had been set for the latest clash between labor and management in Pennsylvania's Anthracite Coal region.

A number of incidents occurred in the late summer of 1897 that led to the trouble that would eventually take place in Lattimer. In August, Gomer James, who worked for the mine owners in a management position, decided to make a central stable for all of the mules who worked in the mines to save money. Mine owners at this time valued a trained mule more than a miner since it cost about $200 to buy and train the animal. One of the savings was that a single crew could now be given the job of feeding and watering the mules. Another consequence of the decision was that the mules were no longer kept at the mines where they worked and the mule drivers had to travel to the central stable to pick them up. In many cases this added two hours to the workers day as they had to wake an hour early to get to the stable to pick up the mule and then spend an hour after work returning the animal. The workers were angry because they received no compensation for this extra time.

On August 13, 1897, a majority of the mule drivers who worked at the Honeybrook mine went on strike. In addition they formed a human fence and refused to allow anyone to enter the mine to get to work. When word of this reached Jones, he grabbed a crowbar, rushed to the scene and attacked the nearest striker, hitting him across the shoulders. The other strikers rushed to intervene and soon had Jones on the ground where they began to beat him. The local supervisor, Oliver Welsh, then intervened stopping the beating and promptly firing all the strikers. In breaking up the fight, Welsh suffered a blow to the head from a stone; it took eight stitches to close the wound.

News of what happened at Honeybrook quickly spread across the coal fields. The result was that more miners joined the strike. Within three days more than 800 miners had joined the effort to better their treatment. They demanded a wage hike, the right to shop at stores other than those owned by the company, the freedom to choose their own doctor and an end to the alien tax. The strikers

ANOTHER TRIAL CERTAIN
FOR SHERIFF MARTIN AND THE OTHER
LATTIMER MURDERERS.

Prosecutors Say the
County's Honor
Demands It.

Jury Feared Coal Barons
and Wouldn't Punish
"Best Families."

VERDICT IN ADVANCE.

So Also Was Judge's Charge.
Sheriff Tells What He'll
Do in Next Trouble.

WHAT *IS* CRIME IN PENNSYLVANIA ANYHOW?

It seems to l settled that in the mining regions deputy sheriffs have the right to kill unarmed strikers on sight. They may pursue them and shoot them down as they would mad dogs. And in the end the deputy sheriffs are glorified as martyrs—not hanged as murderers.

From the New York Evening Journal, 10 March 1898, p. 5

appointed a team of leaders to negotiate with management on their behalf.

The strike ended on a temporary basis when the strikers' leaders negotiated a ten cent pay increase. While the miners were happy with the increase, they remained disturbed that their other issues had not been addressed, and as a result on August 25, 1897, the strike was renewed with a march. Local newspapers reported that anywhere from 300 to 500 miners had taken to the streets to march in protest of their working conditions.

FIRING ON THE MINERS. AN ACCURATE VIEW OF THE FIELD WHERE THE TRAGEDY TOOK PLACE
Drawn by an Inquirer Staff Artist.

By a Philadelphia Inquirer staff person, 12 September 1897, front page.

On September 4, 1879, the miners issued a list of demands. These demands included a fifteen cents per day
raise for every employee, the right to seek out and pay for
the doctor of their choice, they would be paid if they reported to work even if work wasn't possible because machinery
was out of order and they would not be compelled to shop
in company stores or use the company butcher. The coal
companies divided in their response to these demands. By
September 6th the men at Coleraine and Milnesville were
back at work. The mine owners here agreed that the miners could shop where they wished though the company
stores would remain open. That same day, Sheriff Martin of
Luzerne County met with supervisors of the Cross Creek

Coal Company, and it was decided that none of the strikers' demands would be met. The coal company agreed that it would furnish funds to pay for an armed force of deputies to aid the Coal and Iron Police. Sheriff Martin was dispatched to Hazleton with instructions to raise such a force. Martin had no trouble finding men, and within a day, he deputized approximately eighty volunteers who he armed with new Winchester rifles. Martin also issued a proclamation that he sent to the Wilkes-Barre Times. The proclamation put the striking miners on notice in that it warned against any unlawful assembly or any acts of violence.

On September 9th a group of miners from Lattimer met with their counterparts from Harwood. The Harwood miners were already on strike, and the delegation from Lattimer expressed their desire to join in and close both of Pardee's mines in the area. The largely Slavic miners from Harwood agreed that Pardee would give no concessions unless he was faced with a show of unity from the miners. Therefore, it was decided that the Harwood miners would march to Lattimer the next day where the Lattimer miners would join them in the strike.

September 10, 1897, was a warm and sunny day. Approximately three hundred men appeared at Harwood to join in the march to Lattimer. A few of the men carried American flags to display during the march. The vast majority of the marchers did not speak English nor were they American citizens. Michael Cheslock, who did speak English and had applied for American citizenship, was selected to be one of the leaders of the march. The large group set off for Lattimer; they were unarmed and marched peacefully.

As soon as Sheriff Martin received word of the procession, he mobilized his forces. As the marchers neared Hazleton, they were met by Martin and his posse. Martin pulled his gun pointed it at a marcher and ordered the group to disperse. The miners, who felt they were doing nothing wrong, refused. Around this time a fight broke out, and one deputy grabbed a flag from a marcher and tore it to bits. At this point the chief of the Hazleton police intervened. The fighting stopped when the chief said the march

could continue but could not go through Hazleton. The
marchers agreed and proceeded on around the city.

Martin ordered his men to trolleys bound for Lattimer.
Later some of the trolley passengers would report that tensions were high, and there was talk of a shooting. One
deputy was overheard saying "I bet I drop six of them." A
reporter notified the Wilkes-Barre Times that serious trouble was coming. Word of what was happening spread
through the area. Mothers, in Lattimer, went to the local
schoolhouse to remove their children, a wise move in light
of what was about to unfold. The Lattimer mine shut down.
Martin and his men arrived and were joined by coal and
iron police. Now in command of an armed force of about
150, Martin assembled his men at the forked entrance to
the town of Lattimer.

It was 3:45 that afternoon when the marchers approached Lattimer led by a man carrying the American
flag. The miners' ranks had by now swelled to over 400
men. Martin approached the marchers and told them they
were participating in an unlawful assembly. He ordered
them to disperse. Many of the marchers couldn't under-
stand what the sheriff said and just as many could not
hear him. Michael Cheslock and other leaders of the march
attempted to talk with Martin, but the sheriff was having
none of that. He attempted to grab the American flag from
the marcher in front. Failing there, he grabbed a marcher
from the second row, and when other marchers came to
his defense, a scuffle ensued. Martin pulled his pistol, but
it misfired, and at this point someone yelled "fire." Eyewit-
nesses would claim it was the sheriff, but he would deny
the charge. Whoever gave the order, the deputies opened
up. Michael Cheslock was shot between the eyes and killed
immediately. The marchers, seeing what was happening,
turned to run, but the deputies continued to fire. Some ran
toward the schoolhouse where the teachers inside soon
saw shots piercing the walls and sending wood splinters
flying. The shooting went on for at least a minute and a
half, and when it was over 19 of the marchers lay dead and
another thirty-six were wounded. Some of the deputies
walked through the dead and wounded kicking them.
Some of the marchers begged for help, and one eyewitness

heard a deputy respond to these pleas by saying, "we'll give you hell, not water, hunkies!" Sheriff Martin surveyed the area around him, and in a classic understatement muttered, "I am not well."

Wagons were called in to move the dead and wounded to local hospitals and undertakers. Many of the dead were taken to Boyle's and Bonin's who, as undertakers, were assigned the responsibility of preparing the bodies for burial. Undertaker Boyle would later testify that the bodies left in his care had been shot in the back. Boyle's decedents run a funeral home in Hazleton to this day. The funeral director at present is named Thomas Boyle. Tom and the author went to high school together.

The next few days were bedlam in the coal country. Many of the deputies headed to the Jersey Shore to wait out the events. The Governor of Pennsylvania sent the state militia to Hazleton to preserve order since most expected there would be reprisals. To the surprise of many, the immigrants remained peaceful. Large funerals continued in the days to follow, some drawing crowds of as many as eight thousand people.

The story of the massacre was covered in the press throughout the country. Generally the sheriff and his deputies were found to be at fault. *The Philadelphia Inquirer* said that the massacre was,

> "a human slaughter in which men were mowed down like grain stalks before a scythe, by the deadly bullets which stormed for fully two minutes. An exact list of the dead and wounded is impossible to be obtained tonight, but the Inquirer counted twelve dead men in the field. Two others died at the hospital and a number of others are expected to die at any moment."

Sheriff Martin was being hounded by the press, so he finally told his side of the story. He said he received word of the march from one of his deputies who told him that the miners were heavily armed. In response he gathered his deputies together and told them to remain calm no matter what happened. He said when the marchers arrived in Lattimer, he read them the proclamation but that they paid no attention to him and continued to march. Martin said he told the leader to stop, but that order was also ignored. He said he tried to arrest the leader, but when he did, he was surrounded by the strikers who began kicking him. He then told the reporters,

> "I realized something needed to be done at once or I would be killed. I called to the deputies to discharge their firearms into the air over the heads of the strikers, as it might probably frighten them. It was done at once but it had no effect whatever on the infuriated foreigners, who used me so much the rougher and became fiercer and fiercer, more like wild beasts than human beings."

This monument sits at the site of the massacre.

Martin went on to say that the miners were desperate and did not value human life. He claimed that his deputies were ordered to shoot only to protect their own lives and the property they were there to defend. He said that he felt bad about giving the order to fire but insisted that it was his duty in light of the situation.

Soon after this interview, Martin changed his story. He said the marchers were not on company property; that they were on a public road. When asked if the marchers had done anything that was not peaceful, he said no. He denied giving the order to fire saying; that had been done by someone else. Soon after Martin and his deputies were arrested and charged with murder.

The grave site of Michael Cheslock who was the first miner killed during the Lattimer Massacre.

On February 1, 1898, the trial of Martin and his deputies began in Wilkes-Barre. It took over a month to complete and testimony was received from about 200 witnesses. On March 9, 1898 the jury returned with a verdict of "not guilty." News of the verdict sparked outrage not only in the United States but throughout Eastern Europe as well. A Slovak cartoon shows a dead miner laying at the feet of justice. Justice is not depicted as being blind but is seen looking at a bag of money.

In many ways, the martyred miners of Lattimer inspired the working people of America to do something about their working conditions. After the massacre, more than 15,000 workers joined the United Mine Workers of America. In time that union became the most powerful representative of the anthracite workers. At the peak of its power, it represented 150,000 workers in the region.

Here lies 4 of 14 victims of the Massacre who are buried side by side.

In 1972 a monument was erected in Lattimer at the site of the massacre. An inscription on the monument reads,

"It was not a battle because they were not aggressive, nor were they defensive because they had no weapons of any kind and were simply shot down like so many worthless objects, each of the licensed life-takers trying to outdo the others in butchery."

Michael Cheslock is buried in the Hazleton Cemetery. His grave is easy to find if you use the Diamond Avenue entrance to the cemetery. As you enter, Cheslock's grave is to your right just a few yards away from your entry point. Cheslock was 39 years old when he was killed.

If You Go:
Also buried in the Hazleton cemetery is Sergeant Robert H. Sinex who fought with the Union during the Civil War. According to one of his death notices, he was a secret service agent who saw Lincoln's assassination and participated in the capture of John Wilkes Booth. If you wish to visit his grave, we suggest a stop at the cemetery office. The Hazleton Cemetery is located on the same side of Hazleton as the Saint Stanislaus's Polish Catholic Cemetery, and a visit to this site is a must. Fourteen of the miners shot at Lattimer are buried here in a manner to get your attention. The fourteen are lined up side by side against the cemetery wall. Their tombstones are identical and all contain the same information. At the top of the stone is the miners name and inscribed underneath the name on each marker it reads, "Shot September 10, 1897."

This cemetery is located at 652 Carson Street in Hazleton, and the wall you are looking for is the one with the school building right across the street. If you visit Saint Stanislaus's you are right next to the Most Precious Blood cemetery. You may want to stop in here to visit the grave of Jack "the Dandy" Parisi. Parisi was a member of the notorious group Murder Incorporated which accepted and carried out murder contracts from mob bosses throughout the country. A government agent once said of Parisi, "if you hung him up by his thumbs for eight hours he might tell you his name."

If you are in need of refreshments you have plenty of options in Hazleton. We had a pint and the best perogies we have ever tasted at a small pub called the "Battered Mug" located on the corner of South Pine and Beech streets. If you are in Hazleton you are close to many people that we covered within this volume including Jim Thorpe, Black Jack Kehoe of the Molly Maguires, Congressman Dan Flood and Mary Jo Kopechne. As it would be very difficult to visit all the sites in one day, we recommend spending the night at the Comfort Inn located in West Hazleton. The hotel is clean, reasonably priced and has a friendly staff. In addition it houses a nice lounge called "Timbers" that offers live entertainment on the weekends.

These 14 tombstones lined up side by side mark the graves of miners shot to death during the massacre.

"The Man Who Taught America How To Sing"

FRED WARING and
His Band the Pennsylvanians

County: Monroe
Town: Shawnee on the Delaware
Cemetery: Shawnee Presbyterian Church
Address: None listed but anyone in the area will provide directions

Fred Waring was a popular musician, bandleader, and radio-television personality sometimes referred to as "The Man Who Taught America How to Sing." We bet that many of you thought that honor belonged to Mitch Miller. Waring was also the promoter and financial backer of the Waring Blendor, the first modern electric blender.

Fredric Malcolm Waring was born June 9, 1900 in Tyrone Pennsylvania. As a teenager, he formed what became known as Waring's Banjo Orchestra. The band played at fraternity parties, proms, and dances and achieved local success. He attended Penn State University where he studied architectural engineering. He wanted badly to become a member of the Penn State Glee Club but was rejected after auditioning. Waring's Banjo Orchestra became so popular he decided to leave college in order to pursue touring with his band. As it turned out, in Waring's case, leaving the educational world behind proved to be a good move. It appears the entertainment world was ready for his style of music. Waring initially named his band The Pennsylvanians, and they recorded a tune for Thomas Edison called "Sleep." It became their first theme song. The band continued to grow and soon became known as Fred Waring and the Pennsylvanians. From 1923 until 1932, they were among Victor Records best selling bands. In the 1930's, Waring's band had grown to 55 pieces and attained a six month booking at the famous Roxy Theater in New York City along with its very own radio program.

Aside from music, Waring was a talented innovator and businessman. In 1933, Fred Osius invented and patented a

Fred Waring and the Pennsylvanians album cover.

household blender with Waring's financial help. Waring took over the project, redesigned the blender, and launched the Waring Blendor (the "o" in blendor giving it a slight distinction). The blender became popular in the medical field. It was used in the care of patients who had special diets. In addition, the Waring Blendor was utilized by those doing medical research. As a matter of fact, Jonas Salk used it in his development of the polio vaccine. In the mid-fifties, the millionth Waring blendor was sold. It remains a popular item to this day.

During World War II, Waring and his ensemble appeared at war bond rallies and entertained the troops at training camps. He composed and performed many patriotic songs. The most famous of these compositions was "My

America." In 1943, he acquired the Buckwood Inn in Shawnee of Delaware Pennsylvania, renamed it the Shawnee Inn, and made it the center of his musical activities. He created, rehearsed, and broadcast his radio programs from the Shawnee Inn. In doing so, he was able to advertise and successfully market the property.

The year 1943 was a big one for Waring as he also decided to launch his own music publishing company. He called it Words and Music, but later changed it to Shawnee Press. Waring's publishing company soon became one of the largest and most successful in terms of the publishing and sale of choral music. He even formed a male chorus apart from the Pennsylvanians. His approach to choral singing was embraced by the nation. Up until the day he died, he taught and supervised workshops on the subject of choral singing.

During the 1940's and early 50's, Waring and his Pennsylvanians produced a string of hits and sold millions of records. Some of his biggest hits were "You Gotta be a Football Hero", "Button Up Your Overcoat", "Sleep", and "Dancing in the Dark." Waring and the Pennsylvanians grew so popular that in addition to his radio show he moved into television. In June of 1948, "The Fred Waring Show" premiered on CBS. It would run until 1954 and receive multiple awards for Best Musical Program.

Waring also knew it was important to change with the times. In the 1960's as American's tastes in popular music changed, he adapted as well. He formed a group called the Young Pennsylvanians. Members followed the fashions of the times wearing bellbottoms and growing long hair. They performed choral arrangements of currently popular songs. They toured the country and were a popular attraction.

Waring was a big fan of cartoon and comic strips. After being featured in a New York Herald Tribune strip, he invited members of the National Cartoonists Society to the Shawnee Inn as his guests. The artists loved it. Waring would hire buses to provide for their transportation and when they arrived at the Shawnee, all was taken care of. As one of the cartoonists remarked, "he [Fred] had it all." The outing became an annual event held each June for the next 25 years. It resulted in a huge collection of artwork created for Waring by the cartoonists, many of which were turned into table tops at the Shawnee Inn. If you visit the Fred Waring collection at Penn State University today, you can view some of the work. It includes over 600 cartoons and more than 50 of the laminated table tops.

Throughout his life, Waring received plenty of recognition for his musical work, inventions and devotion to the public. He is commemorated by a star at 6556 Hollywood Boulevard on the Hollywood Walk of Fame. Perhaps the most prestigious award was the Congressional Gold Medal he received in 1983 from President Ronald Reagan.

A year after receiving this great award, Fred Waring died on July 29, 1984 after complications following a massive stroke. He was 84 years of age. He had come full circle as the place of his death was Penn State University. He had just completed a workshop on choral singing.

Shortly before he died, Waring designated Penn State to house his collection of archives. The Fred Waring Collection, known as Fred Waring's America, contains the historical memorabilia, music library, recordings, scrapbooks, photographs, cartoons, and business and personal correspondence that reflect his nearly 70 year career as a choral conductor, showman, and pioneer of show business.

Fred Waring lies here without the Pennsylvanians, though no real Pennsylvanian will ever forget his contributions in both the entertainment field and household appliances.

If You Go:

Shawnee on Delaware is a charming town and the Shawnee Inn is still a thriving, picturesque resort. The area is filled with attractions that include live entertainment, skiing, and white water rafting depending on the season. We had lunch at nearby Alaska Pete's Roadhouse Grille and Moondog Saloon on Route 209. The sandwiches were big and tasty and the service was friendly and attentive. It's a stop we would both recommend.

NORTHAMPTON COUNTY

"The Blond Bombshell"
JAYNE MANSFIELD

County: Northampton
Town: Pen Argyl
Cemetery: Fairview
Address: South Main Street

Jayne Mansfield was an American actress who worked on both the Broadway stage and in Hollywood movies. She was born on April 19, 1933 in Bryn Mawr, Pennsylvania. Her name at birth was Vera Jayne Palmer. Early in her childhood, her family moved to Dallas, Texas. It was in Dallas that she spent her formative years. She studied at the University of Dallas and the University of Texas. She spoke five languages and reportedly had a very high IQ. She claimed it was 163. In addition, she was classically trained on both the piano and violin.

While in Dallas, she began to study acting. She was a student of Baruch Lumet, the father of the famed Hollywood director Sidney Lumet. She was also busy winning beauty contests having been named "Miss Photoflash", "Miss Fire Prevention Week," and "Miss Magnesium Lamp."

In the early 1950's, she was working at the Pasadena Playhouse. A Warner Brothers talent scout discovered her and signed her to a contract. Her movie career began with bit parts. Her appearance in movies and her pictorial as the Playboy Playmate of the month in February 1955 turned her into one of the leading sex symbols of her era.

Mansfield's first movie role was in "Female Jungle," a 1954 production. She appeared in a film starring Jack Webb Titled "Pete Kelly's Blues" in 1955. That same year, she returned to Broadway, appearing in the successful play "Will Success Spoil Rock Hunter?" By the next year, she was back in Hollywood starring in "The Girl Can't Help It." This film included performances from early rock stars such as Eddie Cochrane, Fats Domino, and Little Richard. I think we can all agree that a meeting between Mansfield and Little Richard would have been worth seeing.

Actress Jayne Mansfield

In 1957, she reprised her Broadway role for the film "Will Success Spoil Rock Hunter?" The film was a success. As a matter of fact, "The Girl Can't Help It" and "Will Success..." are now considered classics. That same year she appeared in the film "The Wayward Bus" with Dan Dailey and Joan Collins. For her performance, she earned the Golden Globe award as New Star of the Year in the actress category. Natalie Wood was among the other nominees. Unfortunately for Mansfield, she also appeared in "Kiss Them for Me" with Gary Grant that same year. The film was soundly panned by the critics and, as it turned out, was her final starring role for a well known Hollywood studio.

After that, quality roles in quality films were not offered to Mansfield. In 1963, she appeared in "Promises, Promises" where she became the first well known mainstream American actress to appear nude on film. The city of Cleveland banned the movie, though it did enjoy box office success elsewhere.

Though her Hollywood career was floundering she continued to have success in other venues. She appeared on stage in Vegas in a show titled "The House of Love." For her efforts there, she earned $35,000 per week. Even without making films, she was earning anywhere from $8,000 to $25,000 a week for her night club act. She also made a few recordings. In 1965 she released, "As the Clouds Drift By" with "Suey" on the flip side. One of the backing musicians on the recordings was Jimi Hendrix.

At that point in her career, she was also doing television variety shows. She did the popular Ed Sullivan Show and also appeared with Jack Benny, Steve Allen, and Jackie Gleason. She entertained the troops with Bob Hope when he did his tours entertaining the boys overseas. While her film career was over, she was making a great living in the entertainment business.

Mansfield was married three times. Two of her marriages ended in divorce. There were rumors of numerous sexual affairs that included liaisons with men such as John F. Kennedy. She was the mother of five children. One of her children, Mariska Hargitay, is known for her role in the television series "Law and Order: Special Victims Unit."

On June 28, 1967, Mansfield was performing in Biloxi, Mississippi at the Gus Stevens Supper Club. After the performance, she, a male friend, their driver Ronnie Harrison, and three of Mansfield's children who were in the back seat, headed for New Orleans. The party needed to get there that night because Mansfield was scheduled to do a television interview the following morning. At about 2:25

a.m. on June 29th the car carrying Mansfield and her passengers crashed into the rear of a tractor trailer. All three
adults died instantly; the children escaped with minor injuries. Word spread that Mansfield had been decapitated.
This was untrue; she died from fatal head trauma.

Jayne Mansfield is buried beneath a beautiful heart
shaped headstone in Fairview Cemetery in Pen Argyl Pennsylvania. As evidenced by the grave goods (in her case
coins) we found on her tombstone, Mansfield has not been
forgotten. In 1980 the "Jayne Mansfield Story" aired on
CBS. It starred Loni Anderson and Arnold Schwarzenegger.
It was nominated for three Emmy awards.

The sex symbol form the 50's and 60's lies beneath this beautiful tombstone. Note
the grave goods (coins) left for her after all these years. Some guys never forget.

Veterans of the American Revolution and the War of 1812 lie in this old Allentown cemetery.

If You Go:

While there are no other cemeteries of note in the vicinity of Fairview, you are within a half hour of Allentown. Right in downtown Allentown, behind the old Pennsylvania Power and Light building (you can't miss it as it is by far the tallest structure in the city) lies an old cemetery. Within this cemetery lie the remains of many veterans of the American Revolution and the War of 1812.

The authors admit they were perplexed as to how Jayne Mansfield came to be buried in Pen Argyl. As it turns out, we stopped to have lunch in a small diner just outside of Pen Argyl in the town of Gap. We quizzed our waitress but she had no idea who Jayne Mansfield was. She did tell us that there was a gentleman named Charlie in the diner who knew all the local history, and she offered to direct him to our table. We immediately accepted the offer.

Charlie arrived in a flash. We later guessed him to be in his late 70's or early 80's, but he was still in great physical condition, and he appeared to be sharp as a tack. After introducing ourselves we asked about Mansfield. Charlie advised us that Mansfield's mother had settled in Pen Argyl and that she had arranged to have the body shipped there for burial. He also said that Mansfield had other relatives in the area. He then told us he used to have drinks with one of her cousins all the time at the local Legion, until he (Charlie) was banned from the club due to his fondness for foul language.

Charlie asked us why we were interested in Jayne Mansfield and we explained the basis of the book to him. He immediately said, "You boys are doing Mary Jo Kopechne, right?" We had to admit she wasn't on our list, but agreed she should be (See page 34). Our thanks go out to Charlie for the information on Mansfield and for bringing Mary Jo to our attention.

"An Indentured Servant Who Became a Founding Father"

GEORGE TAYLOR

County: Northhampton
Town: Easton
Cemetery: Easton
Address: 401 North 7th Street

George Taylor was a signer of the Declaration of Independence as a representative of Pennsylvania. He was born in Ireland in 1716. As a young man, he wanted to come to America, but couldn't pay his passage so he became an indentured servant to Samuel Savage who ran an iron foundry outside Philadelphia. He arrived in 1736 and started as a laborer, but when Savage discovered that Taylor had a certain degree of education, he made him a clerk in his foundry. In 1742, Savage died and George married his widow, Ann, and took over the iron business. He and Ann would have two children.

He also had five children with his housekeeper Naomi Smith with whom he would carry on an affair for years.

He served in the provincial assembly from 1764 to 1769 and then was reelected in 1775. When problems with Britain surfaced, he immediately spoke out in favor of independence. In July 1775, as colonial forces prepared for war, he was commissioned as a colonel in the Third Battalion of the Pennsylvania militia.

In 1776, the Continental Congress voted for independence on July 2 and adopted the Declaration of Independence on July 4. Before the vote for independence, five of Pennsylvania's delegates, all loyalists, were forced to resign. On July 20, Taylor was among the replacements appointed by the assembly. One of his first duties was to affix his signature to the Declaration of Independence, which he did on August 2. Of the 56 signers, he was one of only eight who were foreign born, the only one to have been indentured, and the only iron master. He was elected to the First Supreme Executive Council of Pennsylvania in 1777 but soon became ill and retired from public life.

Geo. Taylor

After George Taylor resigned from public office, he still continued to support the patriots. From 1777 to 1780, Taylor worked at his iron mills, making cannon balls for the Continental Army. In 1780, Taylor became ill again and decided to return to his home in Easton. He spent the rest of his life there. He died on February 23, 1781 at the age of sixty-five.

Taylor's body was originally buried at St. John's Lutheran Church in Easton. In 1854, a memorial was constructed in the Easton Cemetery for Taylor. In 1870, his body was moved to the site of his memorial and was buried directly in front of it.

If You Go:

Also in Easton Cemetery are the graves of Theophilus Rodenbough, a Congressional Medal of Honor recipient, and James Porter, the Founder of Lafayette College.

Rodenbough (Nov 5, 1838 – Dec 19, 1912) served in the Civil War and was awarded the Congressional Medal of Honor for his efforts at the battle of Trevilian Station, Virginia on June 11, 1864 where he was severely wounded. After he recovered, he lost his right arm at the Battle of Third Wincester on Sept 19, 1864. He also com-manded the 2nd U.S. Cavalry during the Gettysburg Campaign.

This is the tomb of George Taylor a man who lived the American dream.

James Porter (Jan 6, 1793 – Nov 11, 1862) founded Lafayette College. He was a Colonel in the Army during the War of 1812 and served as Secretary of War from 1843 to 1844 during the Tyler Presidency.

Zane Grey as a member of the Penn's baseball team (1895-6)

"Rider of the Purple Sage"

ZANE GREY

County: Pike
Cemetery: Lackawaxen and Union
Address: Lackawaxen

Zane Grey was an American author. He is best known for his adventure novels and stories that presented an idealized image of the old west. While he authored many westerns, his work also includes books about hunting and fishing, six juvenile books, short stories and baseball stories. His best known novel is "Riders of the Purple Sage."

From 1915 to 1924 a Grey book was in the top 10 on the best sellers list every year except 1916. He was published in hardcover, serialized in magazines and reissued in paperback editions. Hollywood turned 46 of his books into movies beginning in 1912 and continuing to the present day. A television series "Dick Powell's Zane Grey Theater" ran from 1956 to 1960 and produced 145 episodes.

When Grey was born in 1872 in Zanesville, Ohio, his parents named him Pearl Zane Gray. His family decided to change the spelling to Grey after his birth. Later he abandoned the name Pearl and used Zane as a first name.

He studied dentistry at the University of Pennsylvania, which he attended on a baseball scholarship, and he graduated in 1896. After graduation he established a practice in New York City. During this period he also played amateur baseball while concentrating on writing in the evenings. He had offers to play professional baseball but turned them down because his burning ambition was to become a writer.

Grey was very close to his younger brother Romer and they frequently fished in Lackawaxen, Pennsylvania on the Delaware river. It was there, in 1900, he met the woman who would become his wife. Her name was Lina Roth but he preferred to call her Dolly. They married in 1905 and moved to a farmhouse in Lackawaxen, where Grey devoted himself to writing full time.

Who would have ever thought that this Rider of the Purple Sage would wind up buried in Pennsylvania?

His first novel titled "Betty Zane" was rejected by every publisher to which it was submitted. He published it himself, but ended up losing money due to the costs. In 1910, Harper's magazine published "The Heritage of the Desert." It became a bestseller and was the prototype of all Zane Grey westerns. Two years later he wrote "Riders of the Purple Sage" which became the most successful western novel ever published.

Despite his success, Grey had problems he had to overcome. He suffered bouts of depression and mood swings throughout his life. One of his coping mechanisms was to engage in his favorite activity, fishing, as it seemed to provide him comfort. When he became financially successful, he indulged in fishing all over the world. This led to regular stories written for "Outdoor Life" magazine that helped popularize big-game fishing.

In 1916, Hollywood bought the rights to "Riders of the Purple Sage." Two years later, the Grey family moved to California to be closer to the film industry and to enable Grey to fish the Pacific. The move proved to be a wise one

"The Mysterious Case of Mary Pinchot Meyer"

MARY PINCHOT MEYER

County: Pike
Town: Milford
Cemetery: Milford
Address: Route 209

She was born on October 14, 1920, in New York City, to a wealthy and politically connected family. Her father was a lawyer active in the Progressive party who contributed funding to the socialist magazine "The Masses." Her mother was a journalist who wrote for magazines such as "The Nation" and "The New Republic." Her uncle Gifford Pinchot was a two time Governor of Pennsylvania (see "Pennsylvania's Forester," p. 80). She would eventually marry Cord Meyer who would go on to work for the Central Intelligence Agency. She would become a friend and lover of President John F. Kennedy. She was murdered in the fall of 1964, and many believe her death was related to her interest in the assassination of President Kennedy. Her name was Mary Pinchot Meyer.

Meyer grew up at the Pinchot family home named Grey Towers in Milford. As a child she met a number of left leaning intellectuals through her parents including Louis Brandeis and Harold Ickes. She was educated at Brearley School and Vassar College. It was during these years that she developed an interest in communism. This did not bother her father at all. He wrote a letter to his brother where he states, "Vassar seems to be very interested in communism. And a great deal of warm debating is going on among the students of Mary's class, which I think is an excellent thing. People of that age ought to be radical anyhow." It was during this period that she first met John F. Kennedy when she attended a dance at Choate Rosemary Hall.

After she graduated from Vassar, Meyer began working as a journalist for United Press. By this time she had joined the American Labor Party. Joining that party resulted in the as, over the years, nearly fifty of his novels were made into more than one hundred movies. Famous actors such as Gary Cooper, Randolph Scott, Buster Crabbe, and William Holden got their start in these films.

Grey became one of the world's first millionaire authors. He wrote more than ninety books, including some that were published after his death. His total book sales are said to be over forty million.

Zane Grey died of heart failure on October 23, 1939 at his home in Altadena, California. He was 67 years old. He is buried in a modest grave, in a small cemetery, in Lackawaken, Pennsylvania called the Lackawaxen and Union Cemetery.

If You Go:

Zane Grey's former home in Lackawaxen is now a museum operated by the National Park Service. It contains memorabilia, photographs, and books in the rooms that served as his office and study. The museum is open on a seasonal basis, usually Memorial Day to Labor Day. Unfortunately, it was not open when we made our visit.

Mary Pinchot Meyer was found shot and killed near her Georgetown home.

Federal Bureau of Investigation opening a file on her political activities. Like her parents, Meyer was a pacifist. In 1944 she met Cord Meyer. Meyer was a marine who had suffered serious combat injuries that resulted in him losing an eye. At the time the two had similar political views and on April 19, 1945, they were married. Shortly after their marriage the couple attended the conference held in San Francisco that resulted in the establishment of the United Nations. Cord Meyer went as an aide to Harold Stassen while his wife covered the conference for the North American Newspaper Alliance.

During this time period the Meyer's started a family. Their first son Quentin was born in 1945, followed by Michael in 1947. The couple had a third son named mark who was born in 1950. With three small children, Meyer settled into the role of being a housewife.

The couple at this time supported the idea of world government. However in 1950 after the family moved to Cambridge, Cord Meyer lost his enthusiasm for the idea. It was also around this time that he began working secretly for the Central Intelligence Agency (CIA). In 1951 he officially became an employee of the agency where he became a key player in "Operation Mockingbird" a covert operation designed to move the American media toward the positions supported by the CIA.

The Meyer family now moved to Washington D.C. and settled in Georgetown. The couple was very visible in Georgetown social circles that included people like Katherine Graham, Clark Clifford and the high ranking CIA official by the name of Richard M. Bissell. In 1953 Senator Joe McCarthy accused Cord Meyer of being a communist. Allen Dulles was successful in defending Meyer, and he was able to keep his position with the CIA. In the summer of 1954 John F. Kennedy and his wife Jackie purchased Hickory Hill a house close to that of the Meyers. Mary Meyer and Jackie Kennedy became good friends and often went on walks together. As the Meyer's political views grew apart, it put a strain on their relationship. In 1956 their son Michael was killed after being hit by a car close to the family home. In 1958 Mary Meyer filed for a divorce. In the filing she alleged "extreme cruelty, mental in nature, which seriously injured her health, destroyed her happiness, rendered further cohabitation unendurable and compelled the parties to separate."

After the divorce Meyer and her two surviving sons remained in the family home. She began painting in a garage at the home of her sister who was married to the *Washington*

Post's Ben Bradlee. In her book *A Very Private Woman* Nina Burleigh, who knew Meyer personally, wrote that during this period Meyer "was out looking for fun and getting in trouble along the way."

During this period Meyer began running into John Kennedy at social functions and parties. Many were aware that he was very much attracted to her, but Meyer knew about his womanizing and for a time that put her off. In addition Kennedy's plans to make a run for the presidency were, by this time well known, and she thought his womanizing was reckless.

After Kennedy's election Meyer evidently changed her mind. Beginning in October 1961, she became a frequent visitor to the White House. The general consensus is that once their relationship became intimate Kennedy and Meyer got together at least 30 times. In addition it is generally believed that on her visits to the White House Meyer brought with her marijuana and in some cases LSD. Meyer during this period told some friends she was keeping a diary.

How close was the relationship between Kennedy and Meyer? In an interview with Nina Burleigh, Kennedy aide Myer Feldman responded to a question with the following, "I think he might have thought more of her than some of the other women and discussed things that were on his mind not just social gossip." Burleigh wrote that "Mary might actually have been a force for peace during some of the most frightening years of the cold war."

In 1976 Ron Rosenbaum and Phillip Nobile wrote an article titled, "The Curious Aftermath of JFK's Best and Brightest Affair." They refer to Mary in the article as the "secret lady Ottoline of Camelot." They claimed to have been granted an interview with a source who did not wish to be identified but was in a unique position to comment on the couple's relationship. The interview went as follows:

"How could a woman so admired for her integrity as Mary Meyer traduce her friendship with Jackie Kennedy?"

"They weren't friends" was the curt response.

"Did JFK actually love Mary Meyer?"

"I think so."

"Then why would he carry on an affair simultaneously with Judith Exner?"

"My friend there's a difference between sex and love."

"But why Mary Meyer over all other women?"

"He was an unusual man. He wanted the best."

In 1983 former Harvard professor Timothy Leary claimed that Meyer visited him and said that she was involved in a plan to avert nuclear war by convincing powerful men in Washington to take mind altering drugs with a goal of having them reach the conclusion that the Cold War was meaningless. According to Leary the purpose of her visit was to find out how to conduct LSD sessions with these men. When Leary suggested that Mary bring the men here so he could conduct the session she responded by saying that was impossible since the man she was involved with was much too powerful.

In her book Burleigh confirms Meyer's own use of LSD and her involvement with Leary which occurred at the same time she was involved with Kennedy. While Burleigh draws no conclusions as to whether Kennedy participated in any LSD sessions she does note that the timing of her visits to Leary coincided with Meyer's known meetings with Kennedy. During a 1990 interview Leary was asked point blank whether he had any doubt that Kennedy was using LSD in the White House with Meyer. He responded by saying, "I can't say that." He pointed out that it was his assumption that Meyer had proposed to take LSD with Kennedy but that he had no proof it had actually happened. Pressed, Leary agreed, that it was possible, even likely, that Kennedy had taken LSD, but he would go no further than that.

On September 24, 1963, Kennedy went with both Meyer and her sister Tony for a visit to the family's Grey Tower estate in Milford, Pennsylvania. The purpose of the President's visit was to dedicate a gift from the Pinchot family to the United States Forest Service. The gift included a large piece of land and the Pinchot mansion which had served as the home of Meyer's uncle and former Pennsylvania Governor Gifford Pinchot. As documented by Peter Janney in his excellent book *Mary's Mosaic* Tony had no idea about the affair between her sister and the President. She said, "I always felt he liked me as much as Mary. You could say there was a little rivalry." Ironically on the same day as the dedication, the United States Senate ratified Kennedy's Limited Nuclear Test Ban Treaty with the Soviet Union and the United Kingdom.

Two months later, after Kennedy was assassinated, Leary said he received a phone call from Meyer who sobbed and said "They couldn't control him anymore. He was changing too fast … They've covered everything up. I gotta come see you. I'm afraid."

There is no way to document where Meyer was when she got word of the assassination. She spent the night at a friend's house in Georgetown. The friend recalled that Meyer was very sad and that they both cried but said very little.

As detailed in Janney's book Meyer spent the next year trying to solve the mystery surrounding Kennedy's death. From the first she was sure it had been a conspiracy, and one of the first people Meyer questioned was Kennedy aide Kenneth O'Donnell. O'Donnell respected Meyer largely because he was aware of the role she had played in the president's life. During one interview O'Donnell said he, "feared she had a hold on Jack." O'Donnell and another Kennedy aide by the name of Dave Powers were riding in the car directly behind Kennedy in the motorcade. Both were combat veterans of World War II. O'Donnell told Meyers about what he and Powers had witnessed that day, the smell of gunpowder and the fact that at least two shots were fired from behind the fence on what has become known as the grassy knoll. Twenty-five years later his account was confirmed by Speaker of the House Tip O'Neill. O'Neill recalled a conversation he had at a dinner with O'Donnell and Powers five years after the assassination. The two told O'Neill that two shots had come from behind the fence. When O'Neill responded, "That's not what you told the Warren Commission." O'Donnell readily agreed saying that the FBI told him it couldn't have happened that way so he testified the way "they wanted me to" because I didn't want to cause more pain or trouble for the family.

Dave Powers was interviewed on the radio in 1991 where he basically told the same story. It was around the time that Oliver Stone's film JFK had been released. After the broadcast Woody Woodland, who had done the interview, was walking Powers to his car when he asked Powers if he had

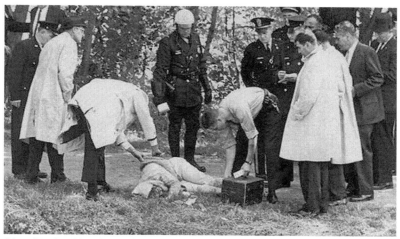

Mary Pinchot Meyer's murder scene

seen the film. He replied that he had. Woodland then asked, "What did you think of it?" Powers responded, "I think they got it right." "Really?" was the reply from a surprised Woodland. "Yes,' said Powers, "we were riding into an ambush. They were shooting from behind the fence." Woodland pointed out that was different from what Powers told the Warren Commission. Powers also admitted that that was true but added he had been told not to say that by the FBI.

Meyer began collecting information on the assassination. One of the people she sought out with regard to the assassination was William Walton, a gay man who had been her escort to many White House social affairs. Walton met Kennedy after World War II, and the two developed a close friendship. Kennedy's wife Jackie enjoyed Walton's company as well and when Kennedy was elected president, Walton enjoyed an almost unchecked access to the White House, and soon he became a close friend of Bobby Kennedy's as well. When Walton met Mary he found her to be distraught with grief. He told her that Bobby suspected something far deeper than Lee Harvey Oswald when it came to the death of his brother. He said Bobby had a plan to take back the presidency, but that it would be years before he could do anything about his brother's death. Despite this information Meyer continued her quest to learn more about Kennedy's death.

In the summer of 1964, Meyer began telling friends that she believed someone had been in her house while she was away. She told another friend that on one occasion she saw someone leaving the house as she was entering. Her friends confirmed that Meyer was frightened by these incidents. By this time Meyer had told a friend, Ann Truitt, that she had kept a diary that detailed her relationship with Kennedy. She asked Truitt to retrieve the diary should anything happen to her.

On October 12, 1964, Meyer was taking her daily walk on the Chesapeake and Ohio towpath in Georgetown. Henry Wiggins a car mechanic was working on a car on Canal Road when he heard a woman scream, "Someone help me, someone help me." Almost immediately he heard two gunshots. Wiggins ran to the edge of a wall overlooking the towpath where he saw a black man wearing a light jacket, dark pants and a dark cap standing over the body of a white woman. Wiggins would later tell police that the man was between 5 feet 8 inches to 5 feet 10 inches and weighed about 185 pounds. According to Wiggins the man turned and looked at him for a few seconds and after shoving something in his pocket turned and walked away disappearing down an embankment.

Meyer's body was taken to the Washington D. C. morgue where an autopsy was performed by Deputy Coroner Doctor Linwood L. Rayford, a man who, by this time, performed more than 400 such procedures on gunshot victims. He found that Meyer had been shot twice: once in the head and once in the back. He concluded that both shots were fired at close range. According to the doctor Meyer probably survived the first shot to the head though it would have rendered her unconscious. He noted that the second shot was fired with remarkable precision. That bullet severed the aorta and death would have been instantaneous. That bothered Rayford because he felt that it indicated that whoever killed Meyer was a professional.

Meanwhile the police had arrested a black man, Ray Crump, who was found in the area of the shooting and who stood 5 foot 4 inches tall. They conducted tests to show that he had fired the gun that killed Meyer but found no nitrates on either his hands or his clothes. They conducted

This modest tombstone marks the final resting place of a woman who refused to believe the conclusions reached by the Warren Commission.

an extensive search for two days that included the use of scuba divers and actually draining the canal near the scene of the murder. No gun could be found. Crump was eventually acquitted (for a detailed account of that story the authors strongly recommend Janney's book *Mary's Mosaic*).

Ann Truitt was in Tokyo when Meyer was killed. She called Meyer's brother-in-law Ben Bradlee and told him about the diary. The next day Bradlee and his wife went to the Meyer home when they arrived it was locked and when they entered they found James Angleton, the CIA counter-intelligence chief already searching for the diary. There are various reports of what happened to it. Some believe Angleton burned it while others believe it remains in someone's possession.

In February of 2001, a writer asked Cord Meyer about Mary Meyer. He responded by saying it had been a bad time because his father had died that same year. Getting back to Mary Meyer the writer asked who could have committed such a heinous crime. Cord Meyer responded, "The same sons of bitches that killed John F. Kennedy."

Mary Pinchot Meyer was laid to rest in the Pinchot family plot in the Milford, Pennsylvania cemetery. She lies next to her son Michael.

If You Go:

Meyer's uncle and former Governor of Pennsylvania Gifford Pinchot (p. 80) is housed in a large mausoleum in the Milford Cemetery. Just across the road from his gravesite is the grave of Charles Henry Van Wyck. He was a New York Congressman, a Senator from Nebraska and a Brigadier general in the Civil War (see page 85).

On February 22, 1861, Van Wyck survived an assassination attempt in Washington. The attempt took place on the same night that an attempt was made to assassinate President-Elect Lincoln in Baltimore. The attack on Van Wyck was apparently motivated by a harsh anti-slavery speech he delivered on the floor of the house. In the speech he denounced the southern states for the "crime against the laws of God and nature." He fought off the attack and survived only because a book and papers that he carried in his breast pocket blocked the thrust of a Bowie knife.

General Daniel Brodhead

Also buried in the Milford Cemetery is General Daniel Brodhead. He fought with George Washington on Long Island and wintered with the Continental Army at Valley Forge in 1777-1778.

"Pennsylvania's Forester"
GIFFORD PINCHOT

County: Pike
Town: Milford
Cemetery: Milford
Address: Route 209

If you have ever been inconvenienced by Pennsylvania's Liquor Laws, or outraged by the cost of alcoholic beverages in the Commonwealth, you can blame, as we will explain later, Gifford Pinchot. The man had an impressive resume. Among the positions to which he was appointed was the First Chief of the United States Forest Service. In addition, he was elected Governor of Pennsylvania twice, first in 1923 and again in 1931.

Pinchot was born on August 11, 1865 in Connecticut. He was educated at Exeter Academy and Yale. His family had made their fortune in the lumbering business. While not opposed to the wealth this had brought him, Pinchot's father grew to regret the damage that had been done to the land. Reportedly, this guilt resulted in him encouraging Gifford to become a forester. His father's influence proved effective, and Pinchot went to France to study forestry. Upon his return to the United States, he found work as a forest surveyor. Pinchot, by this time, had come to believe in the selective harvesting of forest resources. It was his view that forests could produce timber and yet be maintained for the enjoyment of future generations.

In, 1898, Pinchot was named head of the United States Division of Forestry. In 1900, he founded the Society of American Foresters. The establishment of this organization immediately made the forestry profession more credible. In 1905, President Theodore Roosevelt appointed Pinchot to the post of Chief Forester of the United States Forest Service.

Pinchot rose to national prominence under Roosevelt and he remained at his post when William Taft succeeded Roosevelt in 1909. The Taft administration did not view conservation as a priority, and Pinchot found himself in conflict with Richard Ballinger, the Secretary of the Interior. Taft backed his cabinet member and fired Pinchot. The

Gifford Pinchot

firing actually pleased Pinchot as he used it to focus public scrutiny on conservation and forest issues.

In 1910, Pinchot founded and funded the National Conservation Association. He would serve as its president for the next 15 years. The purpose of the organization was to be a watchdog over the use of public lands and to oppose the transfer of public lands back to the states.

In 1912, Pinchot supported the unsuccessful efforts of Teddy Roosevelt and the Progressive Party. Two years later, he ran for Senate under the Progressive Party banner for a United States Senate seat but he was defeated. He put his political ambitions on hold until 1922 when he ran, as a republican, for Governor of Pennsylvania. His main issues were the economy, the enforcement of prohibition, and the regulation of public utilities. He won by a wide margin. His major push, in his first term as governor, was to create a giant power scheme that would result in the transmission of electricity from plants located near the Pennsylvania coal mines. His critics called it socialism but it did appear years later in the form of the Tennessee Valley Authority.

At the end of his first term, he made another unsuccessful attempt at claiming a United States Senate seat. Failing here, he ran for Governor again in 1930 and won. His second term was marked by his efforts to pave rural roads. He also had to deal with the repeal of prohibition in 1933. He quickly called for a special session of the state legislature that resulted in the State Liquor Control Board and the state-run liquor stores. Pinchot's stated intention was "to discourage the purchase of alcoholic beverages by making it as inconvenient and expensive as possible." A majority of Pennsylvanians would say he succeeded.

Here is the final resting place of Pennsylvania's great conservationist and the architect of the Commonwealth's liquor system.

Pinchot ran a third time for the United States Senate and was unsuccessful. In 1938, he made another try for the Governor's office but he was defeated. While he never ran for public office again, he did advise President Franklin D. Roosevelt. In his later years he also wrote a book on his life as a forester, and he invented a fishing kit meant for use in lifeboats during World War II.

Pinchot died from Leukemia on October 14, 1946. He was 81. Several sites are named in his honor including, Gifford Pinchot National Forest in Washington, Gifford Pinchot State Park in Pennsylvania, and Pinchot Hall at Penn State University. The house where he was born, Grey Towers, outside of Milford, is now a national historic site. It is open to the public for tours. It also serves as a conservation education and leadership center. Gifford Pinchot is buried in a large mausoleum in the Milford Cemetery.

If You Go:

Just across the narrow road from the Pinchot gravesite, one can find the grave of Charles Henry Van Wyck. He was a Congressman from New York, a Senator from Nebraska and a Brigadier General in the Civil War.

On February 22, 1861, Van Wyck survived an assassination attempt in Washington. This occurred on the same night an alleged attempt was made on President-Elect Abraham Lincoln in Baltimore. The attack on Van Wyck was apparently motivated by a harsh anti-slavery speech he delivered on the floor of the house. In the speech he denounced the southern states for the "crime against the laws of God and nature." He fought off the attack surviving only because a book and papers he carried in his breat pocket blocked the thrust of a Bowie knife.

Also buried in the Milford Cemetery is General Daniel Brodhead. He fought with George Washington on Long Island and wintered with the Continental Army at Valley Forge in 1777-1778.

Charles Henry Van Wyck

"Traveled Anywhere, Without Fear of Anyone"

CHARLES HENRY VAN WYCK

County: Pike
Town: Milford
Cemetery: Milford
Address: Route 209

Charles Henry Van Wyck was a Dutch American who devoted much of his life to public service. He represented the people of New York as a representative in Congress, the people of Nebraska as a Senator in the United States Senate, and he served as an officer in the Union Army in the Civil War (at the end of which he was brevetted brigadier general). What he is best known for, however, is surviving an assassination attempt motivated by his vociferous opposition to slavery on the same day as an alleged plot against Abraham Lincoln.

Van Wyck was born in Poughkeepsie, New York on May 10, 1824. He graduated from Rutgers College in New Brunswick, New Jersey in 1843. After college, he studied law. He was admitted to the bar in 1847, at which time he opened a law practice in Bloomingburg, New York. In 1850, he was elected District Attorney and served in that capacity until 1856. In 1858, he ran as a Republican for a U.S. House seat and won. He won again in 1860. On March 7, 1860, Van Wyck took the floor in the House of Representatives and delivered a speech denouncing the Democratic Party and its support of slavery. It was one of the most blistering denunciations of slavery ever uttered in the Capitol. He claimed slavery was a crime against the laws of God and nature and violated the instincts of a common humanity. As he concluded, Van Wyck accused Southerners of cowardice and charged them with burning slaves at the stake. Reuben Davis, a Congressman from Mississippi, called him a liar and scoundrel and asked if Van Wyck would "go outside of the District of Columbia and test the question of personal courage with any Southern man?" Duels were illegal in the District and thus the reference to "outside the District." Van Wyck responded, "I travel anywhere, and without fear of any one."

The speech received widespread newspaper coverage and for months afterward Van Wyck received death threats (usually postmarked from south of the Mason-Dixon line).

On the night of February 22, 1861, Van Wyck was returning to his lodgings in the National Hotel after a visit with New York Senator Preston King. As he walked past the north wing of the Capitol he was suddenly attacked by "a stout-built man," as reported by the "New York Tribune." The man seized him from behind and tried to stab him in the chest. The blade cut through Van Wyck's topcoat and likely would have killed him, except that the blow was deflected by a notebook and double-folded copy of the congressional records that were in his breast pocket. As he fought for his life, a second attacker—also with a knife—suddenly appeared. Van Wyck caught the blade with his left hand, punched this second attacker with his right hand (knocking him down), then drew a revolver and shot the first assailant. As the wounded man fell to the ground, a third man sprang out of the shadows and knocked Van Wyck out with a blow to the heat with a bludgeon of some kind. As he fell to the ground, Van Wyck's three attackers ran off.

After regaining consciousness, Van Wyck made it to the National Hotel. Bleeding and groggy, he was treated by doctors as he gave his statement to police. No sign of his attackers was ever found and no motive given. Many, however, felt certain that it was retribution for his speech.

On that same night, President-elect Lincoln was en route to Washington for his inauguration. As he traveled from Harrisburg, Pennsylvania through Baltimore, Allan Pinkerton—founder of the Pinkerton Detective Agency—became convinced that a plot to kill or kidnap Lincoln in Baltimore existed. Pinkerton was hired by the Philadelphia, Wilmington & Baltimore Railroad to protect railroad property along Lincoln's route. According to Pinkerton, his sources reported a plan to have several assassins (armed with knives) interspersed throughout the crowd that would gather to greet Lincoln at the station. When Lincoln emerged to change trains, at least one of the assassins would be close enough to attack.

Memorial to Van Wyck at Gettysburg

In order to thwart this plan, Pinkerton had telegraph lines to Baltimore cut on the evening of February 22 to prevent communication between conspirators, and he had Lincoln arrive secretly in Baltimore in the middle of the night. For the rest of his presidency, the story of Lincoln sneaking like a coward through Baltimore was used repeatedly by his enemies.

Van Wyck recovered from his wounds and remarkably was not at all intimidated by this close call with death. Soon

Van Wyck's grave

after the attack on Fort Sumter, Van Wyck wrote to the White House asking for a military commission. "Those who had talked should act," he wrote. "I desire to be called on at any time no matter what the danger or risk." He was appointed colonel of the 56th New York Infantry, a regiment that he led valiantly until the end of the war. The 56th New York suffered heavy losses at the Battle of Fair Oaks and participated in the Siege of Fort Wagner, South Carolina in July 1863. Later that year, more heavy losses occurred at the Battle of Honey Hill, which was part of Sherman's famous March to the Sea. The regiment was mustered out in October 1865.

In 1866, Van Wyck again ran for Congress as a representative from New York, winning that election and serving until 1871. He moved to Nebraska in 1874 and engaged in agriculture on a farm in Otoe County. He was a delegate to that state's constitutional convention, after which he was elected three times to the Nebraska State Senate. In 1881, he was elected as a Republican to the United States Senate and served there until 1887. In 1892, he ran for governor of Nebraska as a Populist but was defeated. He retired shortly after and settled in Washington, D.C. He died there on October 24, 1895, at the age of 71. He is buried in a rather prominent grave in Milford Cemetery, Milford, PA.

If You Go:

Also buried in Milford Cemetery is Pennsylvania's 29th and 31st governor, Gifford Pinchot (p. 80). He was a noted forestry conservationist and progressive leader, but is also responsible for Pennsylvania's much maligned liquor system.

John Summfield Staples

Stroudsburg Cemetery, in Monroe County (35 miles south of Milford), is home to two noteworthy Civil War figures. John Summerfield Staples was the paid draftee replacement for President Abraham Lincoln. During the Civil War, it became customary to pay substitutes to serve in the army in another's place. Lincoln, hoping to set a good example, selected Staples and offered him a bounty of $500. He saw little action, primarily working as a clerk and prison guard. Also in Stroudsburg Cemetery is John Schoonover. He was wounded three times on the second day of the Battle of Gettysburg while defending against Confederate assaults in the Peach Orchard. He was the last remaining officer in his regiment and, despite his wounds, led his men to a retreat on Cemetery Ridge.

Also of interest 30 miles to the south of Stroudsburg, in Easton (Northampton County), Pennsylvania is the grave of Union Brigadier General Charles Adam Heckman. Heckman served in the Mexican War before the Civil War, and served as Colonel of the 9th New Jersey. He was captured at the Battle of Drewry's Bluff, Virginia and held at the Confederate stockade at Charleston. He was prisoner-exchanged in September 1864. After the war he was a dispatcher for the Pennsylvania Railroad. He is buried at the Easton Cemetery, 401 North 7th Street.

"Why the Hell Not?"
(with apologies to Richie Ashburn)

JAKE DAUBERT

County: Schuylkill
Town: Pottsville
Cemetery: Charles Barber
Address: 140 West Market Street

He used his athletic ability to escape the Pennsylvania coal mines. He had a fifteen year career in the major leagues. He played for the Brooklyn Dodgers and the Cincinnati Reds, and both teams selected him for their Hall of Fames. He played in the World Series twice including the 1919 series that featured the Chicago Black Sox. Twice he led the league in hitting and based on his lifetime statistics one could argue that he deserves to be inducted into baseball's Hall of Fame. His name was Jake Daubert.

Daubert was born on April 7, 1884, in Shamokin, Pennsylvania. His father was a coal miner. When Daubert turned eleven he went to work as a breaker boy. At the time, it looked like he was going to spend his life in the mines much like his father had.

In 1906, Daubert was able to leave the mines when he signed a contract with a semi-pro team located in Lykens, Pennsylvania. Though he began his career as a pitcher, he was soon moved to first base. In 1907 he continued his semi-pro career playing for a team in Kane, Pennsylvania. In the following years, he would play for teams in Nashville, Toledo and Memphis. In Memphis he hit .314, and Brooklyn bought his contract and brought him to the major leagues in 1910, he would play in the majors for the next 15 years.

In his first year in the majors, Daubert hit .264. He would follow this with a number of stellar seasons. In 10 of his major league seasons he hit over .300. In 1913 he won the batting title when he hit .350. That year he was selected the Chalmars Award Winner which would be akin to being the Most Valuable Player today. In 1914 he won the batting title again hitting .329. Though he played in the

Jake Daubert

dead ball era he had power as evidenced by his 165 lifetime triples. Twice he led the league in triples hit. Clearly he was fast of foot as well. In addition he had excellent control of his bat. On August 15, 1914 he set two sacrifice bunt records most in a game (4) and most in a doubleheader (6).

While he was a terrific hitter, Daubert may have been even better in the field. On May 6, 1910 he recorded 21 putouts in a single game just one short of the major league record. Baseball Magazine in 1913 called Daubert "one of the greatest infielders baseball has ever seen." The author

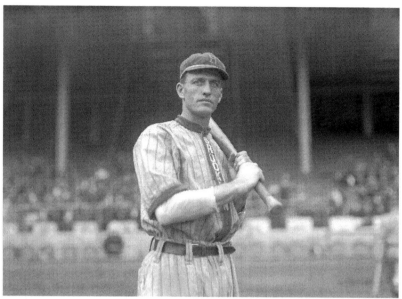

Jake Daubert in 1913.

of the piece also said that Daubert was the most popular first baseman playing the game.

It was in 1913 that Daubert served as Vice President of the Baseball Players Fraternity, an organization working for improved labor conditions. Some believe his actions as a leader of baseball's unionization movement may have played a factor in his not being voted into the Baseball Hall of Fame.

In 1918 Daubert found himself in a dispute with the owner of the Dodgers over money. The season ended early because of World War I, and Charles Ebbets decided not to pay his players for the entire season. Daubert responded by suing Ebbets. While the case was settled out of court, Ebbets had enough, and he traded Daubert to Cincinnati early in 1919. Not only did Daubert become captain of his new team, he helped lead them to a victory in the World Series against the Infamous Chicago Black Sox.

The following three seasons were successful ones for Daubert as he hit over .300 each year. In 1922 he hit for a . 316 average, and he also led the league in triples and hit a career high 12 home runs. He entered the 1923 season as the oldest active regular player in the majors at 39, and he hit .292 that year.

Late in the 1924 season Daubert left the Reds after falling ill. The team doctor performed an appendectomy on October 2nd. There were complications following the operation, and a blood transfusion proved ineffective. A week later Daulbert passed away. Years later Dahlberg's son suffered similar symptoms, and it was found that he had a hereditary condition called hemolytic syherocytosis which probably contributed to his father's death. Daubert was laid to rest in the Charles Barber Cemetery in Pottsville. Among his pallbearers were the Reds manager and some of his teammates.

The side view of Daubert's tombstone.

During his career Daubert compiled a very respectable .303 lifetime average. He still owns the NL

The relatively unknown baseball great Jake Daubert is buried in this Pottsville cemetery.

record for sacrifice hits with 392, and he still second in that category for the major leagues behind Hall of Famer Eddie Collins. When he died he was among the major league career leaders in games played, he was 4th all time in putouts and 5th in assists. He was 7th in career hits with 2,326 and 9th in triples. Certainly the Veterans Committee should consider Daubert worthy of consideration for the Baseball Hall of Fame.

If You Go:

You are not far from the town of Jim Thorpe named for the athlete many consider to be the greatest of all time. The town has constructed a Jim Thorpe memorial which houses the remains of the legendary Jim Thorpe (p. 1). In the center of the town you can pay a visit to the Molly Maguire pub where one can find good food and drink at reasonable prices. At this point you are quite close to the Pocono's so white water rafting and skiing are available depending on the season.

"A Fabulous Dorsey"

JIMMY DORSEY

County: Schuylkill
Town: Shenandoah
Cemetery: Annunciation of The Blessed Virgin
Address: Shenandoah Heights section

In American popular music, Jimmy and Tommy Dorsey achieved that all too rare combination: musical sophistication and vast commercial appeal. The Dorsey brothers were responsible for some of the most memorable music of the swing era. They consistently topped the charts with some of the best rhythms ever recorded. Born in Shenandoah, PA in 1904, James Francis Dorsey was the eldest of the two. Their father was a music teacher in the local high school and tutored the boys in their musical pursuits. He started playing the trumpet and switched to alto saxophone and then learned to double on clarinet. In 1920, he and Tommy, who played trombone, formed their own combo "Dorsey's Novelty Six," one of the first jazz bands to broadcast on the radio. Jimmy also played alone and in big bands and even in pit bands for Broadway musicals.

In 1930 he joined Ted Lewis's band for a tour of Europe. When he returned from Europe, he and his brother kept busy as studio musicians and occasionally co-led an orchestra backing some well-known singers including Bing Crosby. In 1934, they officially formed the Dorsey Brothers Orchestra that included the soon to be famous Glenn Miller. They started recording and soon had some impressive hits such as "I Believe in Miracles" and "Lullaby of Broadway." Many of their songs featured Bob Crosby (Bing's younger brother) on vocals.

Though the two brothers shared leadership, Tommy fronted the band and did most of the work. Jimmy was content to sit with the orchestra and was perfectly happy letting Tommy take charge. Tommy was well known for his temper. He had tremendous drive and often expected too much for those who worked for him. Tommy often resented Jimmy who was easy going and well-liked by the band members. Jimmy was everyone's pal, while Tommy was

Jimmy Dorsey

distant. One night in June 1935 tensions came to a head. Tommy counted off the tempo for their next number, and Jimmy interrupted him saying it was too fast. Tommy didn't say a word but grabbed his trombone and walked offstage, never to return. Everyone asked him to come back, but he refused. The Dorsey Brothers Orchestra became the Jimmy Dorsey Orchestra with vocalists Bob Eberly and Kay Weber. Jimmy Dorsey within a few years emerged as one of the top

In 1947 the Dorsey Brothers, both of whom led highly successful swing bands for more than a decade, sat for this publicity photo for The Fabulous Dorseys, a Hollywood film about their lives and careers. (Image Donated by Corbis-Bettmann)

bandleaders of the day. His brother Tommy now had his own band and a recording contract with RCA Victor and also had a high level of success.

In 1939, Jimmy hired Helen O'Connell as his female singer. She and Bob Eberly projected a boy and girl next door charm, and their pairing produced several of the band's biggest hits. They had eleven number one hits in the 1930s and 1940s. His biggest hit "Amapola" was number one for ten weeks in 1942 on the Billboard pop singles chart. Bing Crosby recorded "Pennies from Heaven" with the Jimmy Dorsey Orchestra, and it went number one for ten weeks and was one of the top records of 1936. In 1957 "So Rare" went as high as number two and was on the charts for 26 weeks. There were movies too. Jimmy Dorsey appeared in a number of Hollywood motion pictures including "That Girl from Paris," "Shall we Dance," "The Fleets In," "Lost in a Harem" with Abbot and Costello, "I Dood It" and "The Fabulous Dorseys."

Amid that string of vocal hits and movies, it's easy to forget that the Jimmy Dorsey band was also a serious jazz outfit, whose members liked to stretch out when they could and just play and leave the vocalist on the sidelines. How good was Jimmy Dorsey? The level of virtuosity he commanded on the alto sax or the clarinet was rated in the same league with Benny Goodman and Artie Shaw.

In 1947 Jimmy and Tommy began to reconcile while filming their quasi-biographical movie "The Fabulous Dorseys."

In 1953, Jimmy and Tommy reunited and formed a new band "Tommy Dorsey and his orchestra featuring Jimmy Dorsey." They gained a good deal of notice for their regular appearances on the Jackie Gleason Show which led to a weakly variety program "StageShow" hosted by the brothers on CBS from 1954-1956. Elvis Presley appeared on several of the telecasts, including his first appearance on national TV in January 1956.

Tommy died in 1956 at the age of fifty-one. He apparently choked to death in his sleep. He was apparently so sedated he didn't awaken when the choking began. Jimmy was devastated by his brother's death and did not outlive him for very long. He passed away seven months later on June 12, 1957 after a bout with cancer. He was 53. He is buried in the Annunciation of the Blessed Virgin Mary

This tombstone marks the final resting place for one of the "Fabulous Dorseys."

Church Cemetery beside his parents. Shortly before his death, he was awarded a gold record for "So Rare" which was recorded in November 1956.

On February 8, 1960 Jimmy Dorsey was inducted into the Hollywood Walk Of Fame. His star is on the North side of the 6500 block of Hollywood Boulevard

In 1983 Jimmy Dorsey was inducted into the Big Band and Jazz Hall of Fame. He is also a member of the American Jazz Hall of Fame. In 1996 the U.S. Postal Service issued a Jimmy Dorsey and Tommy Dorsey commemorative postage stamp, honoring them for their contributions to American music. The Jimmy Dorsey Orchestra has continued successfully for decades and is still in great demand all over the world.

If You Go:
Shenandoah is a small old coal mining town that is very hilly, and it feels like you've stepped back in time. It's the Kielbase Capital of the East Coast and home to Mrs. T's Pierogies. There is a state historical marker dedicated to the Dorsey brothers at Main and Center Streets in Shenandoah.

"The Molly Maguires"
BLACK JACK KEHOE and
FRANKLIN GOWEN

Counties: Schuylkill, Philadelphia
Towns: Tamaqua, Philadelphia
Cemeteries: Old Saint Jerome's, Ivy Hill
Addresses: Corner of High and Nescopeck Streets, 1201 Easton Road

In Pennsylvanian history, there are few groups as interesting or as controversial as the Molly Maguires. Some historians view them as an Irish Catholic terrorist organization, while to others, they are no more than an organized labor movement created as a response to the persecution of Irish coal miners. Still, there are some who argue that the organization never existed. Undeniable, however, is the fact is that between June 21, 1877, and October 9, 1879, twenty Irish catholic men were hanged for murder and accused of belonging to a secret society known as the Molly Maguires. Ten of these men were hanged on June 21, 1877, a day that would become known as "Black Thursday" or "The Day of the Rope."

The Molly Maguire story began in the early 1860's and ended in 1879 when the last hanging took place. The center of action was the anthracite coal region in northeastern Pennsylvania. The alleged Mollies were most active in two counties Carbon and Schuylkill.

As a result of the potato famine in the late 1840's, many Irish immigrates landed in America. Those who settled in the Pennsylvania coal region found that the only jobs available to them were in the mines. The work was difficult and dangerous. In addition, the miners were forced to live in coal company provided housing and could only shop at the company store where prices were so inflated that it was not unusual for a miner to find himself in debt to the company as his wages could not cover his rent and other expenses. These conditions led to the beatings and murder of mine owners, foreman and superintendents. The mine owners and newspapers believed these beatings and

John "Black Jack" Kehoe, "King of the Mollies," soon before his execution in 1878.

killings were part of an organized conspiracy headed by Irishmen who called themselves the Molly Maguires.

During the Molly era, the miners were forming a union under the leadership of John Siney. The union was known as the Workingmen's Benevolent Association and through Siney, and the leadership of the organization as a whole, they sought to seek concessions through negotiations. At

The tombstones in this old cemetery have been destroyed due to vandalism. Two alleged Molly Maguires are buried here including Alec Campbell. Almost all historians agree that one of the two interned here, placed their handprint on his cell wall prior to his execution. The print remains to this day as a sign of his innocence.

times, they used strikes as a tool. In December of 1874, what was called the long strike began in the coalfields. The strike lasted for just under six months and when the miners broke they were forced to return for lower wages than they had previously earned. The person responsible for this settlement was Franklin B. Gowen, the President of the Philadelphia and Reading Coal and Iron Company.

Gowen was born in Mount Airy, Pennsylvania on February 9, 1836. He was the fifth child of an Irish Protestant immigrant who made his living as a grocer. Franklin attended a boarding school, John Beck's Boys Academy, starting at age 9 and ending when he was 13. After serving an apprenticeship to a Lancaster merchant, he decided to study law and worked under an attorney in Pottsville, Pennsylvania which happened to be the county seat of Schuylkill County. In 1860 he was admitted to the County Bar and in 1862 he was elected District Attorney of Schuylkill County. He held this position until 1864 when he resigned in order to pursue a private practice. Among his clients was the Philadelphia and Reading Railroad. He soon left private practice to head that company's legal department. It proved to be a wise move for in 1869, Gowen was appointed acting President of the company.

By this time, Gowen already had the Molly Maguires in his sights. In 1873, he hired the Pinkerton Detective Agency for the purpose of infiltrating the Mollies. Several Pinkerton operatives were sent into the coalfields, including James McParlan, who arrived in Schuylkill County on October 27, 1873, using the alias of James McKenna. In April of 1874, McParlan was initiated into the Ancient Order of Hibernians (AOH), a legal Irish Catholic organization. It was Gowen's belief that the Molly Maguires operated within this organization. It is worth noting that violence on both management's and labor's side increased once the Pinkertons arrived in the area.

The Pinkertons were not the only weapon used by Gowen in his attacks on the Mollies. He had his own private police force known as the Coal and Iron police. An 1868 act of the legislature authorized the creation of this private army. A deputy commissioner for Pennsylvania's Bureau of Labor Statistics held the opinion that the coal operators were their own personal government in the middle of a republic. There was no limit to the number of Coal and Iron policemen that could be hired by the Reading Coal and Iron Company, nor were there any background checks on those who applied to join the force. This police

On June 21, 1877, within the walls of the Schuylkill County prison (pictured above) in Pottsville six alleged Molly Maguires were executed by hanging.

force patrolled the coal region unmolested by local authorities. In May of 1875, Pinkerton sent Captain Robert Linden to the coal fields. He immediately received an appointment as a Coal and Iron policeman. The power of this police force was absolute. They were more powerful than the civil authorities. Linden was instrumental in investigating the crimes that led to the arrests of the alleged Molly Maguires.

One of the most important murders in the Molly Maguire story took place in Tamaqua during the evening hours on July 5, 1875. The Tamaqua police force consisted of two men: Barney McCarron and Benjamin Yost. Yost had a history of running into trouble with an Irish minor named James Kerrigan. Yost had arrested Kerrigan on several occasions for public drunkenness, and in at least one instance subdued Kerrigan with his billy club.

One of the duties of the Tamaqua police force was to extinguish the gas street lights. As Yost was climbing a ladder to shut off one of the light, shots rang out, and Yost fell to the ground. McCarron Turned towards the sound of the shots and saw two forms running away. McCarron gave chase but the assailants escaped. Yost died several hours later and word spread that the murder had been carried out by the Molly Maguires.

The first Mollies that ended up on the gallows were arrested in September of 1875 for the murder of mine superintendent John P. Jones. Jones was shot and killed at a railroad station in Lansford while on his way to work by two men who quickly left the scene. A witness to the murder quickly made the trip to Tamaqua and spread the news. In addition, this man claimed to have seen a man waving something white in the woods outside Tamaqua an apparent signal that brought two other men to him. A posse was formed to investigate. The three men arrested for the crime were found in those same woods having a meal. The men were identified as Edward Kelly, Michael Doyle, and Jimmy Kerrigan. Both Kelly and Doyle carried documents that identified them as members of the AOH. The three were taken to the Carbon County jail in Mauch Chunk, now known as Jim Thorpe.

These initial arrests provided the break the Pinkertons were waiting for, and they quickly took advantage of it. The accused men requested separate trials, and Michael Doyle was the first to be tried. Meanwhile Kerrigan and Kelly were kept in solitary confinement in the county jail.

This initial trial set the tone for the ones that would follow. The jury would have no Irish or catholic members and would be made up largely of Germans, including some who spoke little or no English. The District Attorney, while present, did not try the case. This duty fell to attorneys who worked for the railroad and coal companies. In the Doyle trial the prosecution was headed by General Charles Albright who worked for the Lehigh and Wilkes-Barre Coal Company. The general wore his civil war uniform, including his sword, throughout the trial. One has to wonder how he would have gotten past security today.

The prosecution called more than 100 witnesses that established that Doyle was seen in Lansford on the day of the murder. While no one testified that they had seen Doyle murder Jones, he was described as walking quickly toward the murder site and observed running away with a pistol in hand. The defense did not call a single witness in the case. In their summation the defense conceded that Doyle was in Lansford that day, but he was simply looking for work.

The prosecution case was at its weakest when it came to providing a motive for the murder. Detective McParlan's reports to his superiors laid out a scenario that would have provided a motive. According to the detective, Kerrigan (the head of the Mollies in Tamaqua) had been beaten by the policeman Yost. Another Molly, Hugh McGehan, had been blacklisted by the mine foreman, Jones. Kerrigan initiated contact with James Roarity, the head of the Mollies in Coaldale, in order to exact revenge for these perceived wrong-doings. Kerrigan and Roarity decided that McGehan and a man by the name of James Boyle would murder Yost with the assistance of Kerrigan. Doyle and Kelly, again with Kerrigan's help, would take care of Jones.

The only way the prosecution could introduce this evidence would be to call McParlan as a witness. Because McParlan was still gathering information and the use of his testimony would have exposed his identity as a detective, the prosecution went on without him. It didn't matter. On February 1, 1876, the jury pronounced Doyle guilty and on the 23rd he was sentenced to be hanged.

At later trials, McParlan claimed that it was a common practice among the Mollies to trade jobs. This was done to make it difficult for the townspeople to recognize the out of town assailants.

Something of greater importance to the Molly Maguire story took place during the trial. Jimmy Kerrigan confessed. In fact, he produced a 210 page confession and agreed to testify against his fellow Irishmen in return for immunity. This action earned "Powder Keg" Kerrigan a new nickname, he would henceforth be known as "Squealer" Kerrigan.

Based on McParlan's reports and information supplied by Kerrigan, a unit of the Coal and Iron Police led by Captain Linden made a series of arrests. On February 4th this group set out and arrested James Carroll, James Roarity, Thomas Duffy, Hugh McGehan, James Boyle and Alexander Campbell for the murders of Yost and Jones. Six days later the Coal and Iron Police arrested Thomas Munley as a

Joe Farrell stands in front of Jack Kehoe's grave holding the key supplied by a local resident which allowed us entrance to the aged cemetery. Kehoe has been called the "King of the Mollies" but he was almost surely innocent of the crime that sent him to the gallows.

suspect in the murders of Thomas Sanger and William Uren. Another alleged Molly, Dennis Donnelly, would be arrested later for his part in the murders.

Sanger and Uren were shot and killed on September 1, 1875. On that morning Sanger, who was a mine boss, left for work accompanied by Uren who worked for him. While on the road, the duo was attacked by five heavily armed men who shot and killed them both. Sanger had been targeted for evicting Irishmen. Uren was simply in the wrong place at the wrong time.

Following these murders, a one page handbill titled "Strictly Confidential" began circulating in the coalfields.

Here is Jack Kehoe's Hibernian House looking much as it did the day he was arrested. It is still in operation and run by Kehoe's great-grandson.

The paper claimed to present facts to be considered by the Vigilance Committee of the Anthracite Coal Region. The document goes on to list a number of murders that had occurred in the region and named the murderers and their residences. In terms of the Sanger and Uren case the handbill states, "On September 1st, 1875 at about 7 A.M.

Thomas Sanger, a mining boss, and William Uren, a miner of Raven Run, were shot and fatally wounded by James O'Donnell, alias "Friday," and Thomas Munley, as the unsuspecting victims were on their way to work. Charles O'Donnell, Charles McAllister, and Mike Doyle were present, and accessories to this murder." The information in the handbill was almost certainly based on reports from Detective McParlan, and it is just as probable that it was distributed by the Pinkerton's.

The handbill began circulating in the fall of 1875, on December 10th of that year it would bear fruit. At about 3 in the morning of the 10th Charles and Ellen McAllister were asleep in their home in Wiggans patch. A small child lay between them and Ellen was pregnant. Ellen's mother was also in the house along with her unmarried sons James "Friday" O'Donnell and Charles O'Donnell. Four borders were also asleep in the house including James McAllister who was the brother of Charles.

Charles McAllister was awakened by a crashing noise: the kitchen door being smashed in. He told his wife to stay in bed and ran to the cellar where he made his way to his neighbor's through a door that connected the residences. His wife did not obey; she got up and opened a door that led to the kitchen and was shot and killed. Now pairs of men began searching every bedroom in the house. They brought James McAllister down the stairs into the yard where he freed himself and ran. Shots were fired, and he was hit in the arm but escaped. James O' Donnell also managed to escape. Charles O'Donnell was not so lucky; he was taken outside, and when he struggled free, he was downed by gunshots. Men gathered around his fallen body and emptied their pistols. The shots were fired so close to the body that they burned the flesh. The next day a note was found on the property that stated "You are the killers of Sanger and Uren." Black Jack Kehoe, the man Gowen considered to be the King of the Mollies, was the brother-in-law of both Charles McAllister and Ellen McAllister.

To this day no one knows who the men were who participated in what became known as the Wiggans Patch massacre. What we do know is that Detective McParlan felt responsible. Upon hearing of the killings, he sent a letter of resignation to the Pinkerton office in New York City. In the letter he states, "Now I wake up this morning to find that I am the murderer of Mrs. McAllister." His resignation was not accepted.

Events moved quickly as a series of Molly Maguire trials commenced. The second trial, that of Edward Kelly, began on March 29th. Again, there were no Irish on the jury and the prosecution team was the same. The jury returned a guilty verdict on April 6th, and six days later Kelly was sentenced to be hanged.

After these first two convictions, the Pottsville Courthouse in Schuylkill County was the scene of the next trial. Leading the prosecution in this case would be Franklin Gowen, President of the Philadelphia and Reading Coal and Iron Company. Gowen was well acquainted with the Pottsville Courthouse. As stated previously, he had served as Schuylkill County's District Attorney. The trial started on May 4 and involved the killing of the Tamaqua police officer Benjamin Yost. James Boyle, James Roarity, Hugh McGehan, Thomas Duffy and James Carroll stood accused of the murder.

This trial marked the first appearance of the detective James McParlan as a witness for the prosecution. The informer, Jimmy Kerrigan, would also testify. Just as the trial was getting underway, news spread that the coal and iron police had arrested ten more Mollies in Schuylkill County. Among the ten was Black Jack Kehoe. Kehoe was a respected man active in community affairs who had written to local newspapers denying the existence of an organization known as the Molly Maguires. He was also active in the leadership of the Hibernians. In addition, he had worked his way out of the mines and had much to lose if his leadership of such a group as the Mollies could be proven.

Detective McParlan was the main witness at this trial, and through his testimony, the prosecution was able to leave the impression that the AOH and the Molly Maguires were one and the same. McParlan detailed secret signs and sayings that members used to identify each other. He stated that the chief purpose of the organization was to protect, and, when necessary, seek revenge for members who

On the Day of the rope four alleged Mollies were hanged together at the same time in the old jail in Jim Thorpe. The gallows were built in the middle of the cell block so the condemned men were able to hear the construction prior to their execution.

felt they had been wronged in some manner. In this way he tied the murders and beatings of the mine owners and bosses to the organization. Jimmy Kerrigan also testified and supported McParlan's account.

The defense did call several witnesses in this case including Mrs. Kerrigan who testified that her husband told her he had murdered Yost. She also condemned him for allowing innocent men to take the blame for his crime. While she was being cross examined, one of the jurors became ill. On May 18th the trial was suspended pending his recovery, however his condition did not improve and on May 25th he died of pneumonia. All the work that had gone into the case was lost. The jury was dismissed, and the prisoners returned to the county jail to await a new trial.

Before the second Yost trial began, Alexander Campbell was brought before the court in Mauch Chunk for the murder of John P. Jones. Campbell, like many of the accused Mollies, was born in Ireland. He arrived in Pennsylvania in 1868 where he opened a saloon in Tamaqua. He later moved to the Lansford area where he operated another saloon, the Columbia house. Campbell was viewed by many to be the leader of the Mollies in Carbon County. What made the Campbell trial important was that all agreed he was not present when Jones was killed. He was charged as an accessory before the fact, accused of being involved in the planning of the murder. The prosecution alleged that Kelly, Doyle and Kerrigan spent the night before the killing at Campbell's tavern. The defense countered with several witnesses who said they had been at Campbell's that night and had not seen the three men. After an eleven day trial the jury quickly returned with a guilty verdict and on August 28th Campbell was sentenced to be hanged. Clearly, an Irishman owning a public tavern was a dangerous business to be involved in at the time.

Before Campbell's trial was over, another had begun in Pottsville where Thomas Munley was tried for the murders of Thomas Sanger and William Uren. The prosecution case rested entirely on the testimony of McParlan. Several of Munley's family members testified that he was at home on the day of the murder. Despite this testimony, Munley was found guilty and sentenced to death.

By then, the second Yost trial was underway with the accused being Boyle, Carroll, McGehen and Roarity. Thomas Duffy had requested and was granted a separate trial. McParlan and Kerrigan repeated their testimony and all four men were found guilty. They too were sentenced to be hanged. In addition, the separate trial did not help Duffy as he was also found guilty and received the same sentence.

The Pinkertons continued to investigate past murders including that of mine boss Morgan Powell who had been killed in 1871. Three men, John Donahue, Thomas Fisher and Alec Campbell, were arrested and tried for this murder. All three were convicted and sentenced to death. This was Campbell's second conviction.

The first ten executions took place on June 21, 1877, Black Thursday, or the Day of the Rope as it was referred to by locals. Four of the convicted Irishmen would be hanged in the Mauch Chunk jail. The other six would face the hangman in Pottsville.

The Mauch Chunk hangings occurred first. The gallows had been constructed so that all four men could be hanged at the same time. At around 10:30 in the morning, Alexander Campbell took his place on the gallows. In his final statement, he forgave his executioners. Michael Doyle was next, and he took his spot on the gallows. He said that he had come to this point because of his failure to follow the advice of his church on secret societies. John Donahue took his place and declined comment. Edward Kelly was the last to take his place and, led by his priest, forgave everyone and added that if he had listened to his priests, he would not have found himself on the gallows. The men were then readied for execution and at approximately 10:45, the trap was sprung and the four hurtled to their death. After the bodies were cut down and their hoods removed, the sheriff invited the spectators present to inspect the bodies.

In Pottsville, the authorities had decided to hang the prisoners two at a time. Between 8 and 10 AM, those with official passes were allowed into the prison where they scurried to find the best spots to watch the executions. Meanwhile, the area around the prison, including the hills, were packed with people.

Around 11 AM, the first two prisoners, James Boyle and Hugh McGehan emerged from the jail and made their way to the gallows. Both asked for forgiveness, and Boyle pardoned those who were about to hang him. Ten minutes later, the two were dead. The pair to follow were James Carroll and James Roarity. The latter had been convicted primarily based on the testimony of Jimmy Kerrigan who claimed that Roarity had paid him to have Yost killed. On the gallows, Roarity insisted that this was not so, and he added that Thomas Duffy had nothing to do with the Yost murder. Carroll simply stated that he was an innocent man. Both men were hung at around 12:20. Thomas Duffy and Thomas Munley were the last to the gallows. Neither said much beyond that it was no use and at 1:20, both were sent falling to their death.

At this point the Mollies, if they ever existed, were finished as a power in the coal region. Ten more would be hanged, and others would serve long prison terms. This was not enough to satisfy Franklin Gowen. He wouldn't be happy until he saw Jack Kehoe, who was already serving a seven year prison term, at the end of a rope.

Kehoe was a man who worked his way out of the mines. By 1873, he opened a tavern and rooming house in Girardville called the Hibernian House. He ran this business for three years and during this time became active in local politics. He was elected to the post of Constable in Girardville and was also named Schuylkill County delegate in the AOH. When local newspapers, based on information supplied by the Pinkertons, began linking the Hibernians to the Molly Maguires Kehoe publicly denied such charges. It was Kehoe's view that the Mollies were the fictional invention of the mine owners. Based on information supplied by Detective McParlan, Kehoe was arrested in 1876 and charged with conspiracy to commit murder. This charge did not carry a death sentence, but Gowen resurrected a murder that occurred in 1862 and named Kehoe one of the killers.

Frank Langdon was a mining boss in Audenried where Kehoe lived and worked. On June 14, 1862, he was assaulted by at least three men. He was able to return home, but he died three days later as a result of the beating. In January of 1877, Kehoe was tried for his murder. The evidence presented at the trial was murky at best. Kehoe was said to have threatened Langdon weeks before he was beaten, but other witnesses claimed to have seen Kehoe on a hotel porch at the time Langdon was assaulted. In his summation, Gowen described Kehoe as a man who made money by his traffic in the souls of his fellow men. Despite the lack of evidence, Kehoe was found guilty and sentenced to death.

Kehoe's lawyers fought the conviction to the State Supreme Court which denied the appeal. Next they petitioned the Board of Pardons where they produced sworn statements from John Campbell and Neil Dougherty (both of whom had been convicted of second degree murder in the matter) admitting their participation in the beating and swearing that Kehoe was not present. In September 1878, the Board voted 2-2 on the petition. A tie vote meant the conviction was upheld.

On December 18, 1878, Kehoe waited in his cell with one of his lawyers, Martin L'Velle. He told L'Velle that he was prepared to die. Shortly thereafter, Kehoe took his place on the gallows in Pottsville. Given the opportunity to speak, he proclaimed his innocence, adding that he had not even seen the crime being committed. After making his statement, Kehoe nodded to the sheriff signifying that he was ready. He was quickly shackled and strapped, and at 10:27 a.m., the trap door was sprung. Four other men would be hanged as Mollies after Kehoe, but public interest in the story and in the hangings was never the same. In September of 1978, the Governor of Pennsylvania, Milton Shapp, released a statement that included the following; "It was Jack Kehoe's popularity among the workingmen that led Franklin Gowen to fear, despise, and ultimately destroy him." On January 12, 1979, Shapp signed a posthumous pardon for Jack Kehoe. This is the only posthumous pardon issued in the history of Pennsylvania.

Kehoe is buried in the old Saint Jerome's Catholic Cemetery in Tamaqua. The two victims of the Wiggans Patch massacre, Ellen McAllister and her brother, Charles O'Donnell, were also laid to rest here. The cemetery is located on the corner of High and Nescopeck streets, and it is fenced in and locked. A neighbor who lives on that corner has a key that he is happy to share with visitors. When we were looking for a way in, he appeared and asked "You here to see Kehoe?" That's how we found our way into the cemetery. Two other alleged Mollies, Thomas Duffy and Jack Donahue, are also buried there in unmarked graves. Another place worth visiting in relation to Kehoe is his Hibernian House in Girardville, which is now run by his great grandson. Among the artifacts that can be viewed at this location is Kehoe's cell door from the Pottsville prison.

Alec Campbell is buried in Saint Joseph's Catholic cemetery on Ludlow Street in Summit Hill. There are no grave markers in this cemetery due to acts of vandalism. A mock trial of Campbell was held in Jim Thorpe recently using the transcripts from his trial. A relative portrayed Campbell, and he was found innocent. Another alleged Molly, Thomas Fisher, lies there as well.

The Schuylkill County jail in Pottsville where many of the hangings took place is still in operation, but aside from plaques noting what happened, there is little to see. There is one interesting plaque that is on the wall at the jail's

main entrance. The plaque notes that the largest mass execution in Pennsylvania history took place inside this
prison. It also references the four executions that took
place in Mauch Chunk that same day. What is striking is it
ends by stating that the pardon of Jack Kehoe reflects "the
judgment of many historians that the trials and executions
were part of a repression directed against the fledgling
mine workers union of that historic period."

The Carbon County jail, however, is now a museum
where regular tours are conducted. A replica of the gallows
stands where the original one once stood. In addition, visitors can view the mysterious handprint in cell 17. According to legend, as one of the Mollies (either Alec Campbell or
Thomas Fisher) was about to be taken to the gallows, he
put his handprint on the wall of his cell saying that it
would remain forever as a sign of his innocence. Despite efforts to remove the print, it remains to this day.

Things went well for one of the other main characters in
the Molly story. James McParlan was named manager of
the Pinkertons' office in Denver Colorado. He passed away
in Denver in 1919.

Franklin Gowen eventually lost his leadership position
in the Philadelphia and Reading Coal and Iron Company.
He returned to private practice. On December 13, 1889,

*Final resting place of Franklin Gowen who was the man most responsible for the
hangings of 20 alleged Molly Maguires during the 1870's.*

according to the coroner who investigated the death, Gowen shot himself while staying in a hotel in Washington D.C. Many of Gowen's family and friends believed he was murdered. In 2002, a book written by Patrick Campbell (a descendant of Alec Campbell) entitled "Who Killed Franklin Gowen," concludes that Gowen was a homicide victim. Gowen is buried in the Ivy Hill Cemetery just outside Philadelphia.

In 1969, a highly fictionalized major motion picture called "The Molly Maguires" was released. It was filmed largely in Pennsylvania including several scenes that take place in Jim Thorpe. Much of the movie was filmed in Eckley, not far from Hazleton. Eckley in now a museum and visitors are most welcome. In the movie, Richard Harris plays Detective McParlan and Sean Connery stars as Black Jack Kehoe. It's worth a look.

If You Go:

In the center of downtown Jim Thorpe, you can always visit the Molly Maguire Pub where one can find good food and drink at reasonable prices. The pub has a large outdoor deck that is open weather permitting. That same section of Jim Thorpe is home to many antique and specialty shops that you might want to check out.

In addition, the town is quite close to the Pocono's, so white water rafting is available as well as skiing depending on the season. Finally, you can visit the Jim Thorpe Memorial which is the final resting place for that great athlete (see page 1).

"The Kelayres Massacre"

JOSEPH BRUNO

County: Schuylkill
Town: McAdoo
Cemetery: Saint Patrick's
Address: Lincoln Street

It was election eve in Schuylkill County Pennsylvania in the year 1934. Kline Township Democrats, expecting a big day at the polls in the morning, organized a parade. A local barber named Carl Vacante carried an American flag in front of the marchers who carried red torches. In addition vehicles carrying children were part of the parade. The marchers approached the home of Joseph Bruno a prominent Republican in the area. As they did some of the marchers began to chant "down with the Brunos." Suddenly shots rang out and five of the marchers were killed and many others were wounded. The incident became known as the Kelayres Massacre.

The Joseph Bruno family was active in real estate, bottling beer and politics dating back to the early 1890's. The family had members who held positions such as president of the school board, county detective, justice of the peace and inspector of weights and measures. Joseph Bruno's brother Philip was a tax collector, a Coal and Iron Policeman who also supplied various establishments with slot machines. By 1930 the Bruno family established political control over Kelayres.

Bruno used his position on the school board to enrich himself and his family. The schoolhouse in Kelayres burned to the ground under mysterious circumstances in 1932. The school board that Bruno controlled turned down an offer by a local coal company to rebuild the school. When construction on the new school began the trucks that were used were supplied by Bruno's brothers and Bruno himself acted as the purchasing agent. In that same year Bruno purchased the Lofty School for one dollar. He converted the building into a school bus garage, and the board agreed to rent the building for $30.00 a month.

A parade turned into a bloodbath and became the Kelayres Massacre

Bruno was defeated in the school board election in 1933. However as justice of the peace he impounded the ballots and demanded a recount. Ballots were altered, and they favored Bruno. The controversy over the election led to Bruno's resignation but not before he arranged for his son Alfred to replace him.

Bruno's tenure on the school board was marked by corruption. Teachers were expected to give money to Bruno to keep their positions. By 1934 the teachers had formed a union to oppose the Brunos.

On election eve in 1934 the Brunos remained confident that they would prevail. The local democrats, equally as confident that the tide was turning in their favor, organized the fateful march. The purpose of the march was to signal the end of the 27 year long Republican rule that was headed

The home of Joseph Bruno after the massacre.

by Bruno. Bruno family members occupied homes on two of the three corners at Center and Fourth streets and the democrats decided to March past those homes.

As the marchers approached the homes gunfire rang out. The gunfire came from both sides of the street causing the marchers to scatter in all directions. It was over in about a minute. Three people, William Forke 37, Frank Fiorella 65 and Joseph Galosky 30, died at the scene. Two others Dominic Perna, 37 and Andrew Kostician were rushed to a local hospital. Kostician died the following day, and he was wounded because upon hearing the shots he ran to the scene to search for his daughter. Perna died two days after being wounded. At a minimum 13 other marchers had been hit and required medical attention.

The initial calls to local police were ignored and believed to be prank calls because Bruno was well known and re-spected by the local authorities. When the police did make their way to Kelayres, they witnessed the carnage. They also found an angry mob planning to dynamite the Bruno house-hold. When the police questioned Bruno and the other peo-ple in the house Bruno claimed to have heard shots and that they were aimed at his house. However when the police searched the house they found a shotgun, a pump gun, three doubled-barreled shotguns, three repeating rifles, au-tomatic pistols and revolvers. In addition they discovered a dresser filled with ammunition. Bruno and six other members of his family were arrested.

Joseph James Bruno

In the election held the following day the Democrats swept the state. In Keylares out of 682 votes cast only 24 went to Republican candidates. Democrat George Earle was the first of his party to be elected Governor in decades. He along with a future Governor by the name of David Lawrence would attend the funeral for the five victims of the massacre. The funeral itself drew approximately 20,000 mourners. Many local businesses closed on the day of the funeral including banks, the post office, stores, schools and some of the local collieries. Five hearses took the bodies through the town of McAdoo to their final resting place. As the hearses passed them a number of women screamed in Italian "If you do not send those murderers to the electric chair, we will kill them ourselves."

At the trials the prosecutors produced witnesses who testified that the shots had come from the homes occupied by the Brunos. Witnesses for the defense claimed that the shots came from the home of Dan McAloose who was a local Democratic leader. At his initial trial Bruno was convicted of manslaughter. He appealed the verdict and received a second trial. At that trial Bruno was convicted and sentenced to life while his son Philip was sentenced to ten to twenty years. The other family members were acquitted. However at a third trial both Joseph and Philip were convicted of first degree murder while James, Arthur and Alfred Bruno were convicted of manslaughter.

Joseph Bruno had been convicted and sentenced to three life sentences. He was jailed in the Schuylkill County Prison in Pottsville. Two years later Bruno complained about a sore tooth. A prison guard was assigned to take Bruno to a doctor. Believe it or not when the guard couldn't find a parking place he told Bruno to get out of the car in front of the doctor's office and to wait for him there

Here are the graves of Philip (left) and Joseph Bruno (right). Two men who were considered civic leaders yet opened fire on unarmed marchers killing five and wounding countless others.

while he found a place to park. When he returned to the office Bruno was nowhere to be found.

About eight months later Bruno was found and apprehended lving under an assumed name in New York City. He was returned to the Schuylkill County Prison where he served time for the next ten years until his sentence was commuted. All the others involved in the massacre had had their sentences commuted earlier in the 1940's. Bruno died in Kelayres of natural causes in 1951.

If You Go:

You are very near the center of Hazleton where you can visit a number of sites connected to the Lattimer Massacre (p. 40) including a very sad scene of 14 of the victims of that massacre with their tombstones standing side by side at the Saint Stanislaus's Polish Catholic Cemetery located at 652 Carson Street. We also recommend a visit to the Battered Mug located on the corner of Beech and Pine Streets. We enjoyed the best pierogies we had ever tasted on our visit there. In addition you are close to a number of people we covered within this volume including Jack Kehoe of the Molly Maguires (p. 100) and the man many consider to be the greatest athlete of all time, Jim Thorpe (p. 1). If you visit Jim Thorpe we suggest a visit to the old jail which is now a museum where a number of the alleged Mollies were hanged. In addition you can't go wrong by visiting the Molly Maguire Pub where you will find good food and drink at reasonable prices. Finally the town of Jim Thorpe is very near the Pocono's, so depending on the season you can enjoy white water rafting or skiing.

"The Saddest Affair"

HENRY C. PLEASANTS

County: Schuylkill
Town: Pottsville
Cemetery: Charles Baber
Address: 1400 West Market Street

Henry Clay Pleasants was a coal mining engineer and a brigadier general in the Union Army during the American Civil War. He is best known for constructing an underground tunnel filled with explosives beneath the Confederate lines during the Siege of Petersburg, Virginia, in an effort to break the defense. Following the explosion, the Battle of the Crater ensued on July 30, 1864.

Pleasants was born in Buenos Aires, Argentina on February 16, 1833, the son of a Philadelphia merchant and his Spanish wife. His father smuggled arms and ammunition to South American insurgents fighting against a dictator. After his father died in 1846, 13-year-old Henry was sent to live with his father's brother, a physician living in Philadelphia.

After overcoming a variety of educational difficulties, Pleasants graduated from Central High School with a B.A. in 1851, and then went to work as an engineer for the Pennsylvania Railroad. During these years, he showed a propensity for tunneling and deep mining. In 1857, he moved to Pottsville, Pennsylvania to become a civil engineer in the mining industry. He married in 1860, but his wife died during pregnancy.

When the war erupted, Pleasants enlisted as a second lieutenant in the Tower Guard, a local Schuylkill County unit that became part of the 6th Pennsylvania Volunteers. After an uneventful three months, the unit was mustered out. Pleasants then enlisted as a captain in the 48th Pennsylvania Volunteers, a regiment that was comprised of men from Schuylkill County.

After service on the North Carolina coast, the 48th Pennsylvania was assigned to the IX (Ninth Army) Corps for the remainder of its service. Pleasants saw action at Second Bull Run, Chantilly, South Mountain and Antietam, after which he was promoted to lieutenant colonel.

Henry C. Pleasants

He was wounded in the leg at Fredericksburg, but was able to rejoin his unit for their journey to Kentucky. In July 1863, Pleasants was promoted to provost marshal general of XXIII Army Corps and participated in the Knoxville campaign.

Upon his unit's return to Virginia, Pleasants led throughout General Grant's Overland Campaign during the

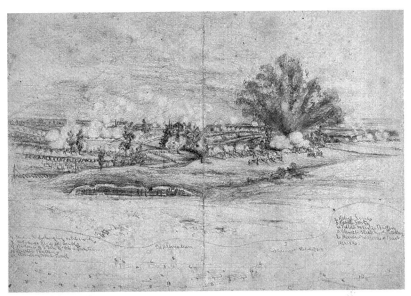

Sketch of the explosion

battles of The Wilderness, Spotsylvania, North Anna River, Cold Harbor and Petersburg.

Many of the 48th were coal miners. During the Siege of Petersburg, Pleasants said he heard his men suggest running a shaft under the Confederate lines and then blowing it up. He took the idea to his superiors, including elaborate drawings he had made. While the plan was approved, Pleasants struggled with a lack of supplies and a lack of interest from the leadership (until, that is, other attacks on Petersburg failed). The plan called for the mine to be detonated between 3:30 and 3:45 a.m. on the morning of July 30, 1864. Pleasants lit the fuse accordingly, but as with the rest of the mine's provisions, they had been given poor-quality fuse, which his men had had to splice themselves. After more and more time passed and no explosion occurred (the impending dawn creating a threat to the men at the staging points, who were in view of the Confederate lines), two volunteers from the 48th Regiment (Lt. Jacob Douty and Sgt. Harry Reese) crawled into the tunnel. After discovering the fuse had burned out at a splice, they spliced on a length of new fuse and relit it. Finally, at 4:44 a.m., the charges exploded in a massive shower of earth,

The crater at Petersburg

men and guns. A crater (still visible today) was created, 170 feet long, 100-120 feet wide, and at least 30 feet deep. The explosion killed nearly 300 Confederate soldiers. However, the Union troops under Ambrose Burnside failed to take advantage of the explosion and suffered considerable casualties. The Confederates counterattacked and soon recovered their original position. General Grant considered the assault "the saddest affair I have witnessed in the war."

After Petersburg, Pleasants remained in command of the 48th until late 1864, but his health was failing. On August 1, 1864, Pleasants was rewarded for his ingenuity and efforts in the tunnel operation; he was promoted to command the 2nd Brigade, 2nd Division, IX Corps, under Brigadier General Robert Potter, the Division Commander, and Major General Ambrose Burnside, the Corps Commander.

Subsequently, on March 13, 1865, the Secretary of War Edwin M. Stanton promoted Colonel Pleasants to brevet brigadier general for his "distinguished services during the war, and particularly for the construction and explosion of the mine before Petersburg." Major General Meade issued a special order thanking Colonel Pleasants and his regiment for this, one of the most extraordinary feats of engineering performed during the war.

After mustering out honorably from the army in 1865 for health reasons, Pleasants returned to Pottsville and resumed his role as a mining engineer for the Philadelphia and Reading Coal and Iron Company, rising to the positions of Chief Engineer and then Superintendent.

Unfortunately, the wartime exposure had affected his health. In 1877, he took a one-year leave of absence to Europe to seek a cure. After a long and lingering dis-

Grave of Pleasants

ease, Henry Pleasants died on March 26, 1880, at the early age of 47. Showing the respect Pleasants had earned, more than 1,000 people attended his funeral. He is buried in the Charles Baber Cemetery in Pottsville, Pennsylvania. Pleasants' tombstone in Pottsville fails to mention his military service, a likely intentional omission on his part.

If You Go:

Also in Pottsville are the graves of:

James Nagle: an officer in the United States Army in both the Mexican War and the Civil War, he is best known for his actions at the 1862 Battle of Antietam, where his brigade played a critical role in securing Burnside's Bridge —a key crossing over the contested Antietam Creek. He commanded a brigade of emergency militia during the Gettysburg Campaign. He is buried in Presbyterian Cemetery in Pottsville (Howard Street at 12th Street).

Jacob Frick: a Medal of Honor Recipient who is also buried in Pottsville's Presbyterian Cemetery. Colonel Frick was awarded the Medal of Honor for his actions at Fredericksburg and at Chancellorsville; and

Nicholas Biddle: buried at Bethel African Methodist Episcopal (A.M.E.) Church Cemetery in Pottsville (816 Laurel Boulevard). Biddle is credited by many as being the first person to shed blood in the Civil War. Born a slave in Delaware around 1796, he escaped to freedom

Nicholas Biddle

by way of the Underground Railroad. Biddle had an interest in becoming a military man, but because he was black he could not be mustered in as a soldier. Not to be deterred, however, around 1840 he became the orderly (an attendant to an officer) of Captain James Wren, the commanding officer of the Washington Artillery, and eventually became so associated with the company and so highly regarded by Wren and the members of the Washington Artillery that he was considered one of their own and even permitted to wear the company's uniform. Responding to President Lincoln's call for 75,000 volunteers to be sent to protect the nation's Capitol less than a week after the first shots were fired at Fort Sumter, the Washington Artillery made their way from Pottsville to Baltimore, where they were to board trains for the final leg of their journey to Washington D.C. On April 18, 1861, while marching through Baltimore to the train station, a large group of Confederate sympathizers quickly gathered around the troops. It was the sight of the then-65-year-old Biddle in uniform that especially infuriated the mob in Baltimore. Racial epithets were hurled in Biddle's direction, soon to be followed by bricks—one of which struck Biddle in the head, causing a wound so deep that a portion of his skull bone was exposed. Biddle survived, and the next day attended remarks given by President Lincoln in Washington D.C. Biddle caught the eye of Lincoln, who spotted Biddle in the crowd and was particularly struck by his appearance (his head being wrapped with blood-soaked bandages). The president urged him to seek medical attention, but Biddle refused, preferring instead to remain with his company. His advancing age and head wound essentially brought an end to Biddle's service. He returned to Pottsville where he would live out the rest of his life. Biddle died at his home there on August 2, 1876, at the age of 80.

INDEX

Cemeteries

Cities and Towns

Pottsville, 90, 93, 103, 110, 112, 113, 115, 121, 123, 127 - 129
Poughkeepsie, 85
Saltsburg, 19
San Francisco, 72
Scranton, 18, 19 23
Shamokin, 90
Shawnee on the Delaware, 52, 54, 56
Shenandoah, 95
South Bend, 15
Stockholm, 3
Stroudsburg, 89
Summit Hill, 115
Tamaqua, 100, 104 - 106, 115
Tokyo, 78
Toledo, 90
Tyrone, 52
Valley Forge, 79, 83
Washington D. C., 34, 35, 72, 74, 77, 79, 83, 86, 88, 117, 129
West Hazleton, 51
Wiggans Patch, 109
Wilkes Barre, 30, 32, 34, 35, 45, 49
Zanesville, 67

Bars and Restaurants
Alaska Pete's Roadhouse Grille and Moondog Saloon, 56
Battered Mug, 51, 122
Molly Maguire Pub, 94, 117, 122
The O'Donnell Winery, 14
Timbers, 51
Woodlands Inn and Conference Center, 22, 29

Made in the USA
Charleston, SC
17 April 2015